"As a firm believer that quality writing can be taught–and learned–I found this book a superb addition to the canon of top-notch guides for both new and practicing authors. It's lucid, insightful and a joy to read." –Jeffery Deaver, international number-one bestselling author

"This book goes beyond the old standbys, offering unique and creative ideas for thwarting writer's block. Great for the beginning writer, as well as the seasoned veteran." –Bob Mayer, NY Times bestselling author

"Finally, a how-to book for writers that doesn't rehash all the familiar exercises. Chris Mandeville has not only filled the pages with tangible ways to break through your crippling moments, but also backed them up with anecdotes from other writers who've put them to work." –Wendy Burt-Thomas, author of *The Writer's Digest Guide to Query Letters* and *The Everything Creative Writing Book*

"A clear, concise, sometimes humorous, step-by-step guide to solving every writer's nemesis...writer's block." –Elizabeth Sinclair, author of *The Dreaded Synopsis*

"Clear, concise, and packed with useful tips. Whether you're facing writer's block for the first time or the fiftieth, Chris Mandeville will help you find a way around it. Highly recommended!" –Nancy Atherton, NY Times bestselling author of the Aunt Dimity mystery series

"Chris Mandeville...distills her teachings into a sort of actionable shorthand. [The] book is crammed with pep talks, pick-me-ups, inspirational tales, but mostly practical actions to replace tired routines or desperation moves. [It's] a guide to help you brainstorm and delve deeper into your process and it gives permission to try a range of tactics to start the words flowing again." –Jessica Page Morrell, author of *Bullies, Bastards & Bitches: How to Write the Bad Guys of Fiction*

"Chris Mandeville's *52 Ways to Get Unstuck* is a must have for every writer's resource library." –New York Times bestseller Dianna Love

"*52 Ways to Get Unstuck* is an exceptionally clear and comprehensive guide to help writers in all stages of the craft. Read it, and you'll get writing!" –Victoria Hanley, award-winning author of *Seize the Story: A Handbook for Teens Who Like to Write*, and *Wild Ink: Success Secrets to Writing and Publishing in the Young Adult Market*

"I've been writing novels for thirty-five years and Chris Mandeville's *52 Ways to Get Unstuck* is the most useful, comprehensive, and entertaining advice on writer's block I've ever read." –Lucia St. Clair Robson, NY Times bestselling author of *Ride the Wind*

"Chris Mandeville's *52 Ways to Get Unstuck* is designed to help with writer's block, but this insightful book also helps writers organize their writing life and offers insights on how to get to a deeper, calmer place to write...If you've ever felt blocked or just needing help to organize your life to have time to write, this is the one book you should own." –Bill Johnson, A Story is a Promise & The Spirit of Storytelling

"There are a ton of great suggestions in Chris Mandeville's *52 Ways to Get Unstuck*. Writers, who need all the help they can get, get that help right here! Highly recommended." –Eric Maisel, *Secrets of a Creativity Coach*

"*52 Ways* gives you a thorough set of tools for staying on track...Clever alignment of the 52 exercises in the book to a deck of cards...invites play as you learn to weave writing into the daily fabric of your life, and this is at root Mandeville's goal: to enlarge the writing life and engage you with the sublime art and craft of making stories." –Lisa Dale Norton, author of *Shimmering Images: A Handy Little Guide to Writing Memoir*

"Buyer beware: Mandeville will deftly dismantle every excuse you've ever used to not write." –Warren Hammond, Colorado Book Award winning author of *KOP Killer*

52 Ways To Get Unstuck:

Exercises To Break Through Writer's Block

Chris **Mandeville**

52 Ways To Get Unstuck:
Exercises To Break Through Writer's Block
First Edition

Copyright © Chris Mandeville 2014 Cover
Design: LB Hayden
PARKER HAYDEN MEDIA
P.O. Box 75881, Colorado Springs CO 80970

In memory of Whisper and Ruh—
The best writing companions a girl could have.

ABOUT THE AUTHOR

Chris Mandeville is a science fiction and fantasy writer who has specialized in getting writers unstuck for almost fifty years (if you count being her dad's muse when she was very, very young). She resides in Colorado with her family, where she is active in the writing community and a frequent speaker at writing events. She served for more than ten years on Pikes Peak Writers' Board of Directors, five of those years as president. Now she is president of Delve Writing, an online community providing writing boot camps, education, networking, and goals support to writers across the globe.

ACKNOWLEDGEMENTS

"Don't go it alone" is writing advice I take to heart, but never more so than when creating *52 Ways to Get Unstuck*. This book would not exist if it weren't for the hundreds of writers I've worked with and learned from over the course of my writing career. Thank you to those many writers, both named and unnamed on the pages of this book, who contributed to the evolution of *52 Ways*, particularly those who participated in the development and testing of the exercises.

I give special thanks to:

Laura Hayden, phenomenal mentor and all-weather pal: you went above and beyond guiding and advising me; I can't thank you enough for your contributions to this book and to my development as a writer.

Pam McCutcheon, generous teacher and friend: your foreword made me blush.

Aaron Brown, business partner, critique partner, and long-time friend: you inspire me to reach higher, work harder, try smarter, and be a better person; thank you in particular for pushing me to write this book.

Deb Courtney, treasured partner in crime: many thanks to you and all the folks at Courtney Literary and the Writing in the Canyon Retreats.

LB Hayden for cover design, Dawn Smit Miller for proofreading, Alicia Howie for formatting, and Parker Hayden Media for selecting this book as the first published under their imprint.

The "NWFs" (non-writing friends): thank you for embracing the insanity that comes with being friends with a writer.

The Sparkling Hammers—my nuclear writing family—who taught me the value of honest, loving critique: Giles Carwyn, Morgen Leigh Thomas, Leslie Hedrick, Aaron Brown, and my first Hammer and steadfast friend, Todd Fahnestock.

Pikes Peak Writers—my extended writing family—for nurturing my growth as a writer.

And last but certainly not least, my actual family: Bill, Nan, and Jessica May, Judy Sawicki, Kathy Santelli, and especially my husband Jody and our children, Duncan, Jack, and Kit. I am grateful beyond words for your love, understanding, and support. I will bake you cookies forever.

FOREWORD

I met Chris Mandeville years ago when she first volunteered to be a part of the Pikes Peak Writers Conference. I remember a friend and fellow board member telling me, "Hey, this lady seems really sharp and enthusiastic. Let's give her some responsibility." We did, and she ran with it—so much so that she poured her heart, soul and considerable creativity into it over the years, eventually becoming the driving force for making the conference what it is today.

Chris has devoted so much of her time to helping writers that this book seems a natural outgrowth of her passion. She knows all too well what it's like to be stuck, to be unable to figure out how to start writing or to solve a problem in a manuscript. Even better, she's come up with fifty-two ways to break through those writing blocks using a simple deck of cards. Don't know what to do? Pick a card . . . any card . . . to try an idea at random. Or read through all of the ideas and choose one that sounds interesting. Some of the recommendations are tried and true methods that writers have used with great success over the years, and some are unique to Chris, but all have the potential to help you pulverize that writing block.

I use some of them already, but I have a problem with actually getting started each writing day and putting my brain in a creative space. So, I'm going to try #4 to create a pre-writing ritual. And, just to get to know my character better, I definitely want to try #19, and the next time I'm stuck, I think #35 might be an intriguing way to find a solution...

No matter what genre you write in, no matter whether you're a beginner or a seasoned pro, if you've ever gotten mired down in your process or your manuscript and can't find a way to pull yourself out of the muck, this book can help you. So, get out a deck of cards and deal yourself a solution!

Pam McCutcheon
Author of *Writing the Fiction Synopsis*
and *The Writer's Brainstorming Kit*

TABLE OF CONTENTS

INTRODUCTION

Being "stuck" as a writer can mean lots of different things. It can mean not knowing what to do next in the plot or when to reveal a critical clue. It can mean not knowing how the heroine should react when she first meets the hero. It can mean writing words you hate and subsequently delete. It can mean the inability to get in The Zone where the words flow easily. It might mean being stuck on a specific element, or it might refer to a general feeling of "everything I write is wrong." It can mean sitting down to write and no words will come. The reasons for being stuck are also varied, including having an overly critical inner editor, feeling too "in love" with our own words, and being unable to focus, among many others.

Ultimately, to get unstuck it's not essential to know *how* you're stuck or *why*. The exercises in this book can help you get unstuck regardless of the details of your personal version of writer's block. In fact, even when you do know the exact reason you're stuck, attacking that problem head-on can sometimes be less effective than coming at it sideways with a random exercise.

Whichever way you're stuck, and whichever approach you take to getting unstuck, the exercises in this book can help you break through your writer's block.

This book is divided into five sections:

**Part One: Clearing the Way to Write—
    Getting Your Life in Order
Part Two: The Right Place at the Write Time
Part Three: Character Juice
Part Four: Story Mechanics
Part Five: Mind Openers—Getting in The Zone**

Whether you decide to select an exercise at random, or to target a specific exercise to combat a specific problem, it's highly recommended that you complete Part One in its entirety *first*.

This is because Part One, Clearing the Way to Write— Getting Your Life in Order, contains five "life prep" activities that help pave the way for a productive writing life. If you attempt an exercise from another section before you've readied yourself and your life for writing, you're not as likely to be successful getting unstuck and staying that way.

After you've completed the prep in Part One, you'll find that Parts Two through Five each contain thirteen exercises for a total of 52.

Why 52?
With 52 exercises, you can use a deck of playing cards to randomize the choice of exercise. There are four categories of exercise, each corresponding to one of the suits in a deck of cards. Each exercise within a category corresponds to a card in that suit.

For example, in Part Three: Character Juice, the thirteen exercises pertain to character. This character category is represented by the "Hearts" suit, and the first exercise in that category corresponds to the "Ace of Hearts." Don't let it trouble you that this is exercise #14 of the 52. There's a chart in Appendix A that shows at a glance which exercises go with which cards.

With any standard deck of playing cards and this handy-dandy chart, you can easily randomize the selection of exercise. Pull a random card out of the deck and do the exercise indicated. Easy-peasy. Or if you decide you want to do exercises from just one category, that's easy too. For example, to choose randomly from the Character Juice exercises, separate all the Hearts cards from the rest of the deck, then draw a card (a Heart) from this subset.

Another Reason for 52

Conveniently there are also 52 weeks in a year, so feel free to process through the exercises one per week over the course of a year. The recommendation to first complete the "Clearing the Way" prep in Part One still applies.

PART ONE:
CLEARING THE WAY TO WRITE— GETTING YOUR LIFE IN ORDER

Writers are often stuck because we haven't cleared our lives and minds for the task of writing. Whether you're stuck right now or simply wanting to prevent becoming stuck, it's a good idea to take stock of your current situation and make changes that will set you up for success.

Often I find that writers whose *job* is to write don't get stuck. They tell me they can't afford to get stuck writing any more than a teacher could afford to get stuck teaching. Imagine a teacher standing idle for hours in front of his class. Imagine what he would say when explaining this to his boss or students or the students' parents:

"I can't teach. I have teacher's block. No teaching will come out."

So why is it okay for a writer to fall back on "I have writer's block" as an excuse not to get the job done? The short answer: it's not. Or at least it shouldn't be.

The following five activities provide practical suggestions for readying your life for writing. You can think of them as "prep" for treating your writing with the same consideration you would any other job (even when you *do* have another job). Doing this prep will pave the way for you to be a productive, successful writer, as well as make it less likely you'll accept writer's block as an excuse not to get the job done.

Freedom to Write

We all have responsibilities, worries, distractions, and "shoulds" in our day-to-day lives. There's a whole lot of "stuff" that can easily come between you and your writing. To achieve the necessary freedom in your life for writing to occur, it's critical to get the non-writing components of your life in order, starting with processing through this check-list:

- Use a calendar to schedule your non-writing obligations.

- Clear time on the calendar to write; move and delete non-writing obligations if necessary.

- Schedule your writing time on your calendar "in pen," i.e., treat it as inviolable.

- If you don't have one, create a place for your writing job. I find it important to have a central, consistent writing hub even if you normally do your actual writing elsewhere. Use it to keep your notes, writing books, print-outs—any and all of your writing-related materials.

- Organize your writing space so it's inviting and easy to find things.

- Provide a way for people to leave you messages without interrupting during writing time, like a white board outside your office. Having people leave text or voicemail messages can work if you're disciplined about turning off your sound notifications when you're writing.

What else can you tidy up or clear away from your non-writing life? Add those items to the check-list, then process through those, too.

If you find you have difficulty mentally letting go of your non-writing life when it's time to write, make it a habit to go through the following steps immediately prior to your scheduled writing time:

- Make a "to do" list of non-writing tasks, then prioritize it.

- For the things that absolutely must be attended to before you can write, do those—and only those— now.

- Give yourself permission to mentally let go of the other things; you don't have to remember or track them because when you come out of your writing fugue, the list will be there to remind you.

- Tuck your non-writing "to do" list someplace safe but out of sight.

- Remove any other reminders of non-writing responsibilities, or go somewhere that has no such reminders.

Don't underestimate the value *to your writing* of getting your non-writing world in order. When we have a handle on our non-writing responsibilities and a way to mentally and emotionally let go of them while writing, we can attain the freedom necessary to get lost in our words. And we all know that's when the magic happens.

For some, the freedom to write is not solely in our own hands. We need "permission" of sorts from others before we can feel comfortable losing ourselves in our writing worlds.

Permission to Write

While "freedom to write" is essentially giving *yourself* permission to write, "permission to write" relates to others—family, friends, coworkers—whose cooperation and complicity is important to your writing success. To achieve true freedom to write, a writer needs for the important people in his life to accept his writing priorities, cooperate with his plans, and respect his sacred writing time and space. Or at least some reasonable approximation of this.

After all, how can a writer "give himself up, body and soul" to writing if the others in his life don't accept that he's off duty from non-writing responsibilities? How can that writer get lost writing if he's worried there will be repercussions when he returns to the real world?

To achieve Permission to Write:

• Let friends and family know you'll be regularly turning off your phone and email during your writing time. Give them a way to contact you in a true emergency (or provide them with an alternate contact, if possible), as well as a way for them to leave you messages for when you're done writing.

- When possible, arrange for someone else to attend to things like answering the phone and the door, and letting the dogs out during your writing time.

- Put up a "do not disturb" sign or other indication that it's writing time.

- Make it clear to others what your expectations are, and what they can expect from you. It's perfectly acceptable to resort to deals, trades, bribes, and rewards.

- Show respect and appreciation. This means adhering to your own rules and timelines, delivering on rewards and promises, and treating your friends and loved ones with at least as much consideration as your writing.

Goals, Plans, Carrots, and Sticks

Now that we have the freedom and permission to write, we're ready to get down to business and write, right? Maybe, but maybe not. What exactly are you going to write? If you're not sure, how do you get started? How do you know when you're done? How do you measure success? When do you celebrate and when do you press that nose to the grindstone a bit harder?

Our next prep task is to articulate our writing goals, both short-term, specific goals and long-term, general ones. After all, in a "real job" it's not usually a secret what your daily goals are, and hopefully you have at least a vague idea of where you want to be in the future.

Your long-term writing goals can be on the order of aspirations and big dreams, like "become a New York Times bestselling novelist." You don't have to specify a timeframe for these goals, and they don't need to be all that practical or even realistic. They should, however, be inspiring and reflect your writing hopes and dreams.

The shorter-term, specific goals should be well-defined, time-bound, measurable, and somewhat realistic, like "complete a 70,000 word rough draft of a cozy mystery by December 31st of this year," and should relate in some way to your dream-goals.

Now to really get down to business: make a plan for how to achieve your goals. To do this, take your specific goal and break it into parts based on how much you need to get done, when it needs to be completed, and how much time you can devote to working on it.

For our "write a 70,000 word rough draft" example, let's say we have a whole year to do that. To begin, break the goal down by month or week: "write an average of 6000 words per month" or "write an average of 1500 words per week." Factor in things like holidays, illness, down days, and emergencies, then create a *daily* plan, like "write 300 words per day, 5 days per week."

Next, take this daily plan and schedule the necessary writing time on your calendar. Resist the urge to jot "3 hours today," and instead choose specific times of day based on your availability, like "Monday, January [date]: 5-6 a.m.; 12-1 (during lunch hour); 1 hour after dinner." I can't stress enough what a difference scheduling your writing time in this way can make to accomplishing your goals.

Now for the fun part. It's finally time to put motivators in place to support and encourage you in attaining your goals. The idea is to motivate yourself to reach your goals by dangling "carrots" to reward you for achievements, and/or "sticks" to punish you when you fall short.

Be open-minded and creative about the carrots and sticks you choose. Experiment and see what works. A big carrot (like a trip to Paris) or a big stick (like a $1,000 donation to a charity you don't like) can work wonders for some, but others find these too distant to provide effective incentive on a daily basis. Consider employing an "immediate gratification" reward/punishment plan for daily progress, like allowing/withholding a favorite television show, a piece of candy, a small gift, or even a "star" or "x" on a progress chart. You can add these small carrots and sticks to a larger, longer-term incentive plan like the trip to Paris.

The efficacy of any given reward or punishment can change over time, so don't be afraid to revisit and replace incentives when you need to re-motivate yourself.

Consider employing the services of an "accountability partner" to dole out the rewards and punishments at specified periodic "performance reviews." As long as your partner is completely immune to your whining and excuses, this can be a valuable technique for keeping you on task.

Don't Go it Alone

> Ask God, your muse, your angels, the ghost of Mark Twain to help you. This job is too big to do on your own.
> — Giles Carwyn, *Heir of Autumn*

Writing is typically a solitary endeavor, and lots of writers go it alone. But the successful ones—the ones who meet their goals, finish books, sell books, and don't suffer crippling writer's block—almost always have support. Sometimes that support is in the form of a friend or partner, sometimes a family or small group of friends, a critique group, club, or writing organization. Whatever form it takes, an effective "writer's support system" provides compassion, understanding, commiseration, and/or love that bolsters and nurtures the writer's soul.

Think about other professions: teachers may stand alone at the front of the classroom, but they have the company and support of fellow teachers, administrators, and students. Even professions you might consider "sole practitioners" have support systems if you look closely. Doctors, lawyers, bus drivers, cosmetologists, chefs, bankers, dog groomers, salesmen—they all have peers, coworkers, colleagues, professional associations and affiliations. Why shouldn't writers?

Find or build yourself some support—a person or group who understands what you're trying to accomplish and wants you to succeed. If they don't understand the pitfalls and nuances of the writer's life, that's okay. Together you can figure out what kind of support you want and need, what kind of system works best for you. Even something as simple as a weekly check-in with another writer or a monthly critique group meeting can help you feel grounded, connected, and supported. From there, there's nothing you can't do.

Show Up

There's no getting around this one. If you don't show up for work, the work won't get done. If you don't get your "butt in chair, hands on keyboard" (or "BICHOK," as it's affectionately known), you won't get your story written. You must show up for work. You must put in the time. If you don't do this, nothing will help you get unstuck.

I'm not a fan of the belief that you must write every day, as I personally do better writing in binges. But when I've been the most successful at getting the work done, and when I've had the least interference from writer's block, is when I've maintained a regular schedule. Granted for me that's a regular binge-writing schedule, like "write for an eight-hour stretch, twice each week," but it is regular, consistent, and enduring.

So whatever your "regular" is, commit to a schedule and stick to it. Put in the time. BICHOK. Show up and keep showing up, over and over again.

PART TWO:
THE RIGHT PLACE AT THE WRITE TIME

Sometimes writers who are stuck are in the wrong place when it's time to write—the wrong mental space, the wrong physical space, or both.

It makes sense that a writer's mental state can play a big role in writer's block, but have you ever stopped to think about how the physical world might be contributing to you being stuck? Or how it might contribute to getting unstuck?

Some exercises in this section address changes you can make to your physical writing environment to help you get unstuck and stay that way.

The other exercises in this section address finding—and staying in—the right mental state when it's time to write.

When it comes to getting stuck, the biggest culprit I've found is the wrong mindset. Specifically this has to do with the difference between the "editor" mindset and the "writer" or "creator" mindset. Let's take a moment to look at these concepts before diving into the exercises.

Writing and editing require different mindsets and different mental skill sets. We use different parts of the brain and different tools for each. While writing is uninhibited, open, flowing, and creative, editing is focused on details and is critical and unforgiving.

I think of the difference like this: writing views the story from the inside; editing views it from the outside.

When a writer is trying to create a story but is stuck in the critical mindset of the *editor*, writer's block is almost inevitable. How can we create any new words at all when the inner editor is censoring and criticizing everything we think of?

We can also get stuck trying to edit our stories when we do so from the creative mindset of the *writer*. How can we cut a single word when our "inner creator" is crying out that each and every one is precious and perfect?

If you think you're stuck because your inner editor won't mind his own business, the best advice I can offer for keeping your "writer's hat" firmly on your head and the "editor's hat" in the drawer is: when you sit down to write, don't re-read your work.

Disclaimer: many writers insist that re-reading their work *actually gets them unstuck*. What's important, however, is what works for *you*. Some people have trouble changing from the "editor's hat" to the "writer's hat." You might not. So give re-reading a try and ask yourself if it puts you into critical-editing mode, or if it stokes your inner creative fires. If you need the "don't re-read" rule in order to stay in the right hat, it's there for your use, no extra charge.

Now I think we're ready for some exercises designed to anchor you (wearing the appropriate hat, of course) in the right place at the write time.

1. WRITE CRAP

Whenever I'm trying to write new words and no words will come, it's because I'm searching for the perfect words to put on the page. This quest for perfection creates a sort of paralysis where I'm censoring my thoughts before they come out of my head.

It's a common enough thing—even recommended—to think before we *speak*, especially when talking to a huge audience and/or people who can change our careers or make us rich, respected, and admired.

"These words are important," we tell ourselves. "It's critical to choose the right words, or we'll look stupid and be laughed or booed off the stage."

But most people who give speeches to a large and important audience don't typically blurt out their words stream-of-consciousness style. They think in advance about what they are going to say. They prepare. They do research. They draft and revise, even if it's only in their heads. The speech they deliver is not their first go at it.

As writers we can sometimes forget that the new words we draft don't have to be fit for public consumption. Just because I write them does not mean they are going to stay that way on the page for everyone to see for all eternity. The words are malleable; they can be changed.

Even as I sat down to write this exercise, I had a moment of paralysis. It was important to me to get this exercise right, so I wanted to choose a great approach, present illuminating examples, and phrase the instructions in a way that immediately brought clarity and understanding to the reader. I wanted each word I typed to be the perfect word. But then I reminded myself: it doesn't have to be perfect on the first draft.

It's okay to write something awful and fix it later.

When I asked horror writer and high school English teacher R. Michael Burns what he does when he gets stuck on a rough draft, he said he reminds himself of the thing he always tells his students: first drafts are allowed to be imperfect.

Burns convinces himself of this truth at least once every time he writes a short story, and had to revisit it multiple times while drafting his novel, *Windwalkers*. His advice: "Just dig in. You can fix it later."

I think multi-published mystery writer Robert Spiller sums it up best: "Write crap."

I agree. Give yourself permission to write crap. I call this "vomit writing," the spewing out of any words that come up. Don't censor yourself. Embrace the crap! Let the words flow out of you, the worse the better.

Write. Write anything. Write nonsense. Write crap you know you'll throw away. Write whatever comes into your head. If you keep doing it, the juices flow. I've never had writer's block since I found this.

— Matt Bille, *The Dolme*

2. *IMPROVISE*

Nothing banishes the inner editor like a session of improv writing. Like improvisational acting, improv writing is off-the-cuff, not pre-planned, not practiced, uncorrected artistic expression.

I learned about improv from a group of writers that meets at a bookstore each week to do improv writing together. Their process is that the leader provides a prompt to the group, then each writer immediately— without any prep or planning—works individually writing something inspired by that prompt. There is a time limit and a requirement that everyone reads their work aloud when time is up. There is one strict rule: no criticism. No critique of any kind.

The time limit and requirement to read your work are essential. Together they force you to write something, *anything*. The prohibition against critique is also key. It gives you permission to write something awful, as long as you write something. This forces you to push past insecurities, make decisions (even if they turn out to be "wrong"), and ignore the inner critic.

Writing improv in a group is incredibly freeing and unbelievably fun, so I encourage you to find a group or create your own. But you don't need to have a group for this to work. There are plenty of books and Internet sources where you can find prompts to write to on your own. Or you can create your own list of prompts, cut it into strips with individual prompts on each, and put them in a box to draw from. Better yet, swap a box of prompts with a writing friend.

Once you've mastered this kind of "vomit writing," use it without prompts to spew out new words for whatever story you're writing.

Author M.J. Brett had great success using this process to get unstuck when she was writing *Between Duty and Devotion*. She says she couldn't decide if her protagonist, Sara, would fly to New York to help another character, Neil, recover from surgery when it meant risking a job she loved. After trying many other methods to figure this out, M.J. finally solved the problem by writing whatever came to mind about Sara without stopping to correct anything. In the process of this "free-writing," as she calls it, she realized that Sara would go to New York to help Neil, no matter the repercussions. Since then, M.J. free-writes the rough drafts of all her novels without worrying about finding the exact right word or stopping to correct spelling or do research.

> The free-writing cleared the air and made me concentrate on character instead of editing.
> – M.J. Brett, *Truth Lies Six Feet Under*

Give improv or free-writing a try. It may take a while to get the hang of it, but keep at it until you are able to bypass your inner censor and spew words straight from the creative center of your subconscious mind. Keep the pen flowing across the page, or the fingers flying across the keyboard, and write. Write, write, write. Though you will likely find that you occasionally produce beautiful writing this way, it doesn't matter what the product is—it's the *process* that's invaluable to getting unstuck.

3. CHOOSE YOUR READER

By asking you to choose your reader, I'm *not* suggesting you figure out your target market or actually select a friend to read your work. I don't mean an actual reader at all. Instead I'm referring to an imaginary reader, a reader that exists only in your mind.

In *Unstuck: a Supportive and Practical Guide to Working Through Writer's Block,* author Jane Anne Staw, Ph.D., says that writers consciously or unconsciously have a particular reader in mind when we write. Do you? Who is the person—real or fictional—that you imagine reading your work? Is it your father? Your high school English teacher? Your thesis advisor from college? Your spouse? Your critique partner? Your boss?

Fantasy writer Bonnie Hagan is well aware of her inner reader. His name is Spike and he looks an awful lot like the villainous gremlin from the 1980's movie *Gremlins*. This super-critical, mean-spirited font of negativity stands on Bonnie's left shoulder and watches her work, constantly reminding her that everything she writes is total and utter garbage, that she doesn't have an ounce of writing talent in her whole body, that she's an idiot to think she could be a writer, and she should just give up.

Luckily Bonnie's right shoulder is occupied by a different reader: a four-inch tall blond cheerleader. She's peppy and positive, and has a "B" on her uniform for Team Bonnie. She loves everything Bonnie writes and encourages her to keep writing no matter what. Bonnie does her best to block out Spike and write for the cheerleader. It's a constant battle, but one she's determined to win.

If your imaginary reader has become an unforgiving inner critic, how can you bring yourself to write down a single word, or be happy with anything you write? Staw says to mentally choose an approving inner reader. Imagine yourself writing for your favorite teacher, your minister, your grandmother. If you don't have a real person in your life like that, pick someone from history or fiction who fits the bill. Or write for Bonnie's cheerleader.

4. RITUALIZE

In much the same way that children wind down to go to sleep better when they have a bedtime ritual, writers can gear up to write (or revise) with a ritual that achieves the right mindset for writing (or revising).

Most writers I know have some kind of limited routine or series of steps they go through before writing. Some are aware of their habits, some not until asked to think about it. Sometimes the pre-writing routine is more ritualized—the exact same things in the exact same order—while sometimes it's a more casual approach. A beverage is almost always involved: tea, coffee, Mountain Dew, wine, absinthe, and on the rare occasion water.

> First step: black tea. I brew a couple of liters a day and make it last into the evening. Usually Singell Estate Darjeeling, but there are several others I like, too. No sugar or honey, just pure tea. Hot, of course. I gather a variety of V5 Pilot Precise pens (black, purple, blue, light blue, green, red, pink), and I start by reviewing what I wrote the day before and marking any changes/corrections needed. By the time I've finished that and I'm well-caffeinated, I'm

> already into the story and moving forward. The
> caffeine keeps me energized all day, and once
> I really get into a scene, it's harder to get back
> out than to stay in and work.
>
> – Martha Gilstrap, *Slitherskins*

Children's book author Maria Faulconer has a very specific pre-writing ritual. She's a "morning person" and gets up early, while it's still dark outside and the house is quiet, to take advantage of her heightened creativity during that time of day. She brews a pot of tea and heads to her writing space. There she lights a candle with a long match, focusing on the intensity of the flame for a moment while she sets an intention for her writing session. Finally she puts on some soothing music, usually soft piano, and begins to write. She finds that this simple routine centers and grounds her in a way that helps her focus on her story. If she's ever stuck, going through these steps is often all it takes to get her back in the right mindset.

For me, whether I'm writing a first draft or doing revisions, I need to remove everything from my mental and physical space that draws me away from writing. That means I do the chores around me that are nagging, or go to a space where I can't "see" chores. I attend to emails that absolutely can't wait, then turn off my email program, along with all the other programs on my computer except for word processing. If after this I still feel concerned or preoccupied with non-writing tasks, I make a list of all the things I need to do after my writing time, then I tuck the list out of sight. Finally I get a very large, very hot cup of coffee and I open my manuscript document.

While my ritual is the same whether I'm writing or revising, you may find it useful to have a different routine before editing than before writing because of the different mindsets required. For example, re-reading the chapter you worked on the previous day might work well when you're in editing mode, but when you're writing a first draft it could serve to stifle your creativity by engaging your inner critic.

When creating a pre-writing ritual for yourself, there are no required elements (unless you count the anecdotal evidence of a beverage). Rather, your routine should be unique to you, designed to produce the mindset you need in order to write. Think about the way you want to feel when writing or revising, and employ actions that typically evoke those emotions in you. Want to feel energized? Perhaps go for a run. If you're typically anxious, consider meditating or taking a shower to relax. If you're easily distracted, think about things that help you focus: yoga, composing intentions, reading your personal mission statement or logline, clearing your desk.

Whenever possible, select elements for your ritual that can be employed at any time or place. If you must touch the north wall of your office four times before writing, that will make it difficult to write anywhere else. But if saluting the north direction will suffice, you can do that anywhere, walls or not.

Think also about the length of your ritual. I suggest making it as short as you're able without compromising results. That way you have more time to write. Keep in mind, too, the possibility of compressing or expanding the ritual based on how you're feeling at the time—if you go for a walk to get the story ideas flowing, you can shorten or lengthen it to fit your daily circumstances.

Once you identify a routine you think will achieve your desired state, try beginning each writing session with that ritual for ten days. Is it working to get you centered? Is it helping you to be more productive? Can you shorten it and still achieve results? As long as the ritual is working for you, there's no need to change it. But if you ever find you're not in the right mindset after your ritual, rethink your routine with an eye to optimizing each element to achieve the results you desire.

5. PROP YOURSELF UP

Go sit where you write most often and take a look around. Do you see anything that might jolt you out of writing mode, like a "to do" list or a treadmill? Is there anything that makes you feel less than perfect, like a rejection letter or an unflattering photograph? Anything that nags at you to take care of it, like a dirty tank full of hungry, neglected fish or a stack of paperwork?

Get rid of it. Get rid of it all. Put the bills in a box so you can't see them. Stash the "to be filed" pile in an empty file drawer. Give the fish to your neighbor kid or put them in another room. Remove the family activities calendar from sight. Put away absolutely everything that does not bolster, support, or enhance your writing life or your positive image of yourself.

If it's not possible to completely clear away the accouterments of your non-writing life, make yourself a new writing space, either by going to a different room or making a partition with a tall bookcase or a room-dividing screen. If you don't have a writing space of your own, now is the time to carve out a special spot dedicated to writing and personalized to suit you. You deserve it, and your writing will benefit.

Once you've stripped your space of things that detract from your writing, start adding things that will enhance your writing: framed memorabilia, a piece of art, your favorite sweater, a plant or fresh flowers. What you add is subjective. Only you can say what enhances and what detracts from your focus on your writing and your emotional buoyancy. The point is to keep your personal demons at bay by surrounding yourself with objects and images that enhance your self-confidence, your creativity, and your concentration.

Some writers I know frame their rejection letters and hang them on their office walls because rejection spurs them to fight harder, write longer, do better. However I find visible evidence of my own failures to be discouraging, so I prefer to display awards and the like in much the same way that author Anne Hillerman keeps fan letters nearby to read when she needs a boost.

Romance writer MK Meredith enhances her writing space with collages that depict the direction and success she desires for her career. In creating her collages, she goes through magazines cutting out photos that represent her writing dreams, scenery that represents her deepest yearnings, and words that evoke emotion, challenge, and motivation, including those that evoke in her the emotions she wants to evoke in her readers, which she describes as "an emotional ride on heated sheets." She looks for anything (be it pictures, words, or colors) that inspires her, anything that reminds her why she writes, why she continues without hesitation after rejection, why she can't imagine doing anything else. She glues these clippings to a poster board, frames it, and hangs it on her office wall directly across from her writing space. If she's ever stuck, she gazes at the collage. Sometimes to get unstuck all she needs to do is to immerse herself in her stories, but sometimes she has to look more closely at the individual collage elements to find the inspiration to continue writing.

Although MK focuses on collages that depict her overall writing journey, she highly recommends creating collages for individual manuscripts. They're a great way to get to know your characters and can provide powerful, specific inspiration during writing days that feel less than inspired.

Adorning your walls with collages and memorabilia is great at home, but what if you need to venture out into the world to write? It's awkward to lug framed certificates of achievement to your local coffee shop, and it's not always convenient to bring poster board collages to the picnic table at the park. What then?

Kirsten Akens, who is a journalist as well as a blogger, recommends a modern twist on MK Meredith's collage technique that works well for writers on the go. She uses the Internet site Pinterest to compose collage boards for her works-in-progress. She suggests that fiction writers, in particular, create one board for each character, as well as boards for setting, theme, and other elements. (And those boards can be "public," for friends' or critique partners' input, or kept "secret.") Not only is every image on the Internet available, but Kirsten likes that Pinterest allows her to access her boards from any computer anywhere she writes.

Another suggestion is to condense down a whole office worth of positivity into a portable prop. I prefer a prop that makes me feel good about myself in general, rather than a prop that symbolizes a story. One small item can symbolize all the fan letters and awards and mementos of past successes. This can be as simple as an image on your computer, a sticky-note on your journal, a piece of jewelry, or a travel mug.

This type of "feel positive" prop is very personal, so do some inner detective work to ascertain what symbol will best work for you and your needs. If your great-grandmother bequeathed you a ring that makes you feel cherished and generally good about yourself, then wear it whenever and wherever you write. You can carry an "I won NaNoWriMo" water bottle or a "Best Dad Ever" coffee mug to remind you of your successes. Wear a bracelet that says "writer" or a necklace with an inspirational charm. Post your personal motto or a special affirmation on your writing surface. Write a message on the back of your hand.

It may be more difficult to capture the essence of your story in a prop than it is to create a symbol of positivity, but it can be done. Make a small, easy-to-carry collage, choose a journal with a cover that evokes the theme of your story, customize the background image on your laptop screen, or get one of those cool do-it-yourself mugs that has a slot for you to place a photo or drawing behind clear plastic.

Whether you select one prop or you surround yourself with a host of specially chosen items, make sure you peek at them as often as needed to prop yourself up. Use them to remind yourself you are doing a good job. Use them to inspire you when you are out of ideas. Look at them any time you need to remember what you are trying to accomplish.

6. LEAVE THE NEST

> Changing the place you write is a great way to change-up and often "charge-up" your writing energy. Take a break from your desk and change your surroundings. Get a new perspective with a new landscape. Take a blanket and go to a park. Enjoy the breeze as you sit in the grass and write a description of the town where your story is.
>
> – Jennie Marts,
> *Easy Like Sunday Mourning*

One of the easiest and most effective things to do to get unstuck is to go somewhere else. No matter how inspiring, supportive, comfortable, and positive your regular writing space is, sometimes it's best to leave the nest. Sometimes simply changing your physical environment to *anywhere different* can flip a switch inside you that removes the block. Other times, however, it takes a bit more planning and calculation to make this happen.

Try the easiest thing first: go to another place in the same room, or another room in the building. If you're outside, go in. If you're inside, go out. Pick somewhere convenient and try writing. This worked for author F.T. Bradley:

> When it was time to write *Double Vision: Code Name 711* (the second book in the series), I just couldn't get going on the first draft. I tried to write early in the morning, late at night, but the words weren't making the page—I was writing too slow to make my deadline. Then (more out of desperation than anything) instead of writing at home, I started writing while my kids were in class, at the nearby food court. Without Internet or domestic duties to distract me, I was writing up a storm. I just had to change where I wrote to get unstuck—who knew?

If your first attempt at writing somewhere different doesn't get you unstuck, take a moment to evaluate the nature of your block and make a calculated change to your environment that addresses the problem head on. For example, if you are physically uncomfortable in your old desk chair, and your aches and pains keep bumping you out of your story world, borrow or buy an ergonomic chair. Or if you're having a hard time getting into the mindset of your protagonist in your stranger-in-a-strange-land story, maybe you feel too safe and comfortable in your usual surroundings, and you should go somewhere strange and foreign. This is similar to what happened with Shannon Lawrence when she was trying to write a horror short story. The sights and sounds and smells of her house were so familiar and comforting, she couldn't get into the right mindset to set the tone for her story, so she went to a café she'd heard about but never been to. It wasn't a horror-themed café, but simply being in a new and foreign place did the trick:

> The lack of anything familiar helped me narrow my focus down to the screen in front of me. There was something about the isolation from my everyday life that helped me key into my work and let the story fly. I was only there for a couple hours, but I was so engaged with the story that I hammered out the entire thing, finishing the rough draft as I sat there. Not only did I get unstuck, I did good work—this story was accepted by the first magazine I submitted it to.
>
> – Shannon Lawrence, "The Blue Mist"

So, little birdies, if you're stuck perhaps it's time to fly the coop.

7. HUMAN SAFETY NET

In order to get unstuck and *stay* unstuck, you might benefit from a writing partnership, a goals group, or a live cheerleader (someone whose opinion you respect). The purpose of forming this type of relationship is to build accountability for your writing in a safe, positive environment. You want a partner who will motivate and encourage you, not criticize you; someone you can talk with about your woes without fear s/he will make you feel worse than you already do. Someone who will push, cajole, bribe, tempt, threaten, or coerce you into getting past a block.

To begin this relationship, it's a good idea to make an agreement or contract that clearly defines what each party wants out of the partnership. Make sure it's safe for you to say anything you are thinking or feeling about your writing. Be clear about what types of responses you desire. For example, the contract might specify that when you're down or stuck, the other person reminds you you're a good writer, points out when you're wearing the wrong hat (editor/writer), and/or suggests techniques to help you get past stumbling blocks.

The important thing is to figure out what kind of input has a positive effect on you, and what's detrimental. If you respond well to certain reminder phrases, like "remember that it always takes you a week to get over a rejection letter," you should absolutely arm your partners with this information. If there are certain phrases they should never utter, be sure to tell them these as well. For me, when I'm stressed the worst thing my writing partner can say is "relax." That only serves to make me angry on top of being stressed out.

Sometimes members of a critique group can function as a safety net, encouraging and supporting each other when they're down or stuck or behind schedule. However sometimes a critique group may not feel like a safe place to confess fears or admit to being stuck due to the critical nature of the critique process. My critique group, however, could not be more helpful. I can always go to them for advice, and support if I'm stuck or feeling low. If you don't feel comfortable forming a support system with the members of your critique group, consider joining or forming a "goals and accountability group" with other writers either in person or online.

If you have one close friend—writer or not—who is willing, consider trading a reward and/or a punishment with him/her to give you incentive not to stay stuck. If you meet your goal, the other person doles out your reward. If you don't meet your goal, you get the punishment.

A great example of a motivating punishment is practiced by science fiction writer Margaret Yang with the help of her co-author (they write together as M.H. Mead). Margaret sets a writing goal for a specific period of time. She tells her co-author the goal and hands over a donation check made out to a political party or candidate that Margaret *detests*. If Margaret doesn't meet her goal on time, her co-author mails the check.

Margaret says she learned this technique from Chris Baty's book *No Plot? No Problem!* Baty provides instructions for this method, which he calls "conditional donations" and credits to writer Paul Griffiths. Margaret has used it for a number of years and finds it a painful enough consequence to keep her pushing through blocks. She's pleased to report that she hasn't missed a goal yet.

Another great incentive is having an enthusiastic reader who is waiting for your work. When Alicia Howie was writing *Seven Days of Grace*, she gave her beta reader each chapter as soon as it was written. This reader loved the story so much, if Alicia took too long to get her a chapter, the reader would nag her until she came through. Since this reader was also Alicia's boss, when Alicia got stuck she had increased incentive to push through and find a solution or else risk angering her employer. As an added bonus, since the boss wanted the story as soon as possible, Alicia could sometimes get away with writing during work hours.

If you work better with carrots than with sticks, arrange to receive a reward when you meet your goals. The bigger the goal, the bigger the reward. But don't neglect to incentivize the smaller, short-term goals, too. A trip to

Hawaii when the book sells is terrific to strive for, but it may be the bottle of Scotch you get when you complete a chapter that keeps you pushing forward when you're feeling stuck.

8. GROUP DATING

When you're stuck, gather some writer buddies and write in parallel. If you like you can begin the date with social talk, then move into talking about what you're going to write. Write for an hour, then stretch and chat a little, then write for another hour. Merely sitting in the presence of other writers who are working may help get you in the right mindset to write. If you get stuck during the date, you know that help is only the next break away. If you make this group date a regular occurrence, it should eventually become a quick and easy trigger for slipping into the writing groove.

Mentally it can be a big help to have a "date" to write (whether it's with a group, one friend, or just with yourself) because when you have an appointment to do something, and you know that's what you are *supposed* to be doing, you don't have any "shoulds" in your head about doing something else.

A *writing* group—not *critique* group—is a great way to make a date with yourself to write and be held accountable for actually doing it. Sometimes that's all it takes to get the creative juices flowing.

J.A. Kazimer is a prolific writer. *Usually*. But recently

she had a terrible case of writer's block. She says she was stuck "in a big-picture way" in that she couldn't get started on the next book in her series. She couldn't muster the energy or will to write, even though the deadline was looming over her.

She agreed—out of desperation—to try this group dating exercise to see if it would provide the jump-start she desperately needed. She attempted to schedule the date with her writing buddies, but could not find a time when everyone was available. She confessed that she wasn't all that disappointed about this, however, because said writing buddies were *not* stuck. In fact, they were each writing every day, and the thought of facing them added to J.A.'s discouragement.

Fortunately as her deadline loomed larger, J.A. had a commitment to teach a writing class:

> I didn't go into the class with the "group dating" idea or expectation, but once I was there it developed naturally from the situation. My students, while being smart and good writers, hadn't been writing for long. They hadn't reached the burnout stage of revision or word count that I had. Instead they were *eager*, which was when I realized the value in starting my project while in the midst of their energy and enthusiasm. So I did. As always, by the time I started writing, I was invested. I no longer felt exhausted, the word count no longer felt daunting, and I was excited about writing again. To get there took breaking out of my rut, and allowing the company of others to propel my words.
>
> – J.A. Kazimer, *The Assassin's Heart*

9. SKIP AROUND

Sometimes when you think you're stuck, it's possible you're not completely blocked but rather just stuck on a particular page or scene. Don't get locked into thinking you have to write scenes in order. Skip ahead ten pages, ten scenes, or even ten chapters and see how you do there. Going to a different section may be all you need to get back in the groove. When you go back to the original sticking point, chances are you won't feel stuck anymore.

Deb Buckingham, author of *Dishcloth Diva*, says that when she can't push through a chapter, she skips ahead to the next one and writes that. Invariably this helps her figure out what should happen in the place where she was stuck, then she goes back to fix it.

Sometimes it can be helpful to skip all the way to the end of the story, then leapfrog your way back through the major plot points to the trouble spot. This is an especially helpful technique when you get stuck writing a mystery or thriller.

Author Laura Hayden often employs a process she calls "reverse engineering." She developed this method when she was struggling with a particularly complex murder-mystery whose due date to the publisher was rapidly approaching. In a "light bulb moment," she realized that when she shelved books at her bookstore, she was faster and more accurate if she went in reverse alphabetical order, and she wondered if the same principle would apply to plotting. She gave it a try and plotted the murder backwards, starting with who committed the crime, when, where, and why. Then she created the characters who did *not* commit the crime but who would be logical suspects, fleshing them out with motives, opportunities, and means. By working the mystery in reverse order, she saw more clearly where to plant diversions, distractions, misunderstandings, bald-faced lies, additional crimes, and "red herrings." After reverse engineering the plot, she got the book written in record time and made her deadline.

So if you find yourself stuck at one place in your manuscript, try skipping around. You may find yourself skipping for joy.

10. KILL A BUNCH OF BABIES

Sometimes when writers are trying to make revisions, we discover we are so in love with our "babies" (the words we've created), we can't achieve the objectivity necessary to determine which words are essential and which ones should be cut.

If you're stuck this way, print out a scene and get rid of every word that's not absolutely necessary. Line through the words so you can still read them, then make a new computer file with the changes, but don't delete the original version. Take a break from that scene for an hour, a day, or longer. If possible, don't look at the story at all during this time.

When you have a little distance from the project, read the new version without looking back at the original. As you read, what is noticeably missing? Add in details if you think they're essential to moving the plot forward, showing a character trait, or making the story understandable to a reader. When you're done, if you feel your cuts have made the "magic" disappear from the page, you always have the older version to refer back to.

Let's try this method on a paragraph I wrote:

Cate looked around at Heaven. It was barren and dusty and brown. Nothing like she'd imagined it to be. No green grass, no rainbows or blue skies. No angels or puppies or waterfalls. Instead of the smell of her favorite daffodils, the musky scent of greasewoods hung over the mesa like it had just rained, but the earth was parched and there wasn't a single raincloud in the endless grey sky. Cate didn't feel renewed or rejuvenated. She felt exhausted and weighted down. Not at all like she'd just been set free of all her earthly fears and responsibilities. She wanted to bury her face in her hands and sob and cry it out, then sleep for an eternity, but instead she hauled herself to her feet, dusted off her jeans and looked around. Maybe somewhere in Heaven there was someone who could tell her why her mother had done what she'd done to her so long ago.

Do you see unnecessary words? Let's line them out:

Cate looked ~~around~~ at Heaven. It was barren and ~~dusty and~~ brown. Nothing like she'd imagined ~~it to be~~. No ~~green~~ grass, ~~no~~ rainbows or blue skies. No angels or puppies or waterfalls. Instead of the smell of ~~her favorite~~ daffodils, the musky scent of greasewoods hung over the mesa like it had just rained, but the earth was parched and there wasn't a ~~single rain~~cloud in the ~~endless grey~~ sky. Cate ~~didn't feel renewed or rejuvenated. She~~ felt exhausted and weighted down. Not ~~at all~~ like she'd ~~just~~ been set free of ~~all~~ her earthly fears and responsibilities. She wanted to bury her face ~~in her hands~~ and sob ~~and cry it out~~, then sleep for an eternity, but instead she hauled herself to her feet~~, dusted off her jeans~~ and looked around. Maybe somewhere in Heaven ~~there was~~ someone ~~who~~

could tell her why her mother had done what she'd done to her ~~so long ago~~.

After removing the lined-out words, here's what we end up with:

Cate looked at Heaven. It was barren and brown. Nothing like she'd imagined. No grass, rainbows or blue skies. No angels or puppies or waterfalls. Instead of the smell of daffodils, the musky scent of greasewoods hung over the mesa like it had just rained, but the earth was parched and there wasn't a cloud in the sky. Cate felt exhausted and weighted down. Not like she'd been set free of her earthly fears and responsibilities. She wanted to bury her face and sob then sleep for an eternity, but instead she hauled herself to her feet and looked around. Maybe somewhere in Heaven someone could tell her why her mother had done what she'd done to her.

Is that better? Sure. But did we really take out everything that wasn't necessary? No, not by a long stretch. Let's try again.

~~She looked at~~ Heaven. ~~It~~ was ~~barren and~~ brown. ~~Nothing like she'd imagined. No grass, rainbows or blue skies. No angels or puppies or waterfalls. Instead of the smell of daffodils,~~ the ~~musky~~ scent of greasewoods hung over the mesa like it had ~~just~~ rained, but ~~the earth was parched and~~ there wasn't a cloud in the sky. Cate felt exhausted~~ and weighted down.~~ Not like she'd been set free ~~of her earthly fears and responsibilities.~~ She wanted to ~~bury her face and~~ sob then sleep ~~for an eternity~~, but ~~instead~~ she hauled herself to her feet ~~and looked around~~. Maybe ~~somewhere in Heaven~~ someone could tell her why her mother had done what she'd done ~~to her~~.

Here's what we end up with this time:

```
    Heaven was brown. The scent of greasewoods hung
over the mesa like it had rained, but there wasn't
a cloud in the sky. Cate felt exhausted. Not like
she'd been set free. She wanted to sob then sleep,
but she hauled herself to her feet. Maybe someone
could tell her why her mother had done what she'd
done.
```

Okay, that's pretty sparse. I'm not sure how we could pare that down further without losing the meaning. Are we done? No way. That pared-down paragraph may have the same bare-bones meaning as the original, but it's lost the voice, the nuance, the flavor, the detail. I think we need to put some words back, don't you? Not all of them, but a few.

```
    Heaven was brown. The musky scent of
greasewoods hung over the mesa like the tail end
of a rain, but the earth was parched and there
wasn't a raincloud in the endless grey sky. Cate
felt exhausted. Weighted down. Not at all like
she'd just been set free of all her earthly fears
and responsibilities. She wanted to bury her face
in her hands and sob, then sleep for eternity, but
instead she hauled herself to her feet. Maybe in
Heaven someone could tell her why her mother had
done what she'd done.
```

I did put back some filler words like "instead." That word isn't essential to the meaning of the sentence, but I didn't think the sentence conveyed a strong enough contrast with "but," so I added "instead" back in. Likewise "bury her face in her hands" is not needed, but I like the image more than simply "sobbing."

You may not agree with these choices. You might not think that the last paragraph is better than the previous ones. Not everyone would make the exact choices I did. But the point is that *I* considered the choices, thought about them carefully, and made purposeful decisions. There are no words that accidentally slipped in. If a word is in that final paragraph, it's because I made a conscious decision to include it. I think this process gave me more objectivity about my work, which made the final product stronger.

If you're having trouble editing because every word seems precious and perfect, give this exercise a try. You may find that some words and phrases you considered essential are actually not. Or you may still find yourself thinking that your writing—or at least 98% of it—is fabulous as-is. If this happens, it could be that your words *are* perfect. Or it could be that you are simply unable to gain the perspective needed to make cuts that would improve your work.

If this happens, please don't jump straight to the conclusion that your words are perfect. Ask for help. Have another person do this exercise with your scene. Or have one person do the cuts and a different person add detail back into the sparse version. You don't have to adopt their changes, but try to see the work through their objective perspectives. It can be an eye-opening experience, especially if your helpers know nothing about your story to begin with.

When you're done I hope you'll have gained some measure of objectivity about your work, at least enough to see that sometimes a word is a just a word, and not a baby at all.

11. Use a Time Machine

When writers have trouble moving forward in the editing phase, often it's because we're afraid of losing our work. The fear of replacing something good with something worse can be paralyzing. The key to overcoming this stumbling block is to save everything. Devise a titling and filing system, and save your work with a new title before you edit. This way you can "go back in time" to a previous version of your story any time you want. Then you can be free to hack away at the current version without fear that you are permanently destroying a word, phrase, paragraph or scene you may want later.

When multi-published author Evangeline Denmark signed the contract for her book, *Curio*, the publisher requested she change the time period from the future to circa 1900, a task so daunting she froze in her tracks. She knew she had to do *something* if she was going to meet her deadline, so she made a copy of the manuscript, then tucked the original safely away and started making changes to the copy. Knowing she could go back to the original at any time gave her the courage to experiment with the new time period, adding and cutting and changing details to see what worked.

In one illustrative example, Evangeline had a paragraph that revealed an essential part of a character's arc while vividly describing that character looking out a screen door. However some research on the history of screens revealed that it would be highly unlikely for her character to have a screen on her back door given the new time period. Evangeline couldn't keep that paragraph.

> But the image I created was so poignant—I hated to give it up. I tried rewriting the paragraph, using flapping laundry in the place of the torn and fluttering screen, but it didn't work. The magic of the simile was gone. So I cut the entire paragraph and showed the necessary character development in a different way. I was only able to cut that paragraph because I knew it was preserved in its original, heart-rending detail in my other document. If I decide later that I want to try to restore the paragraph to the manuscript, I know my beautiful screen door word picture is saved and available.
>
> – Evangeline Denmark,
> *The Dragon and the Turtle*

Once you've completed revisions on a copy of your manuscript, if you go back and read an earlier version, it will most likely be obvious to you how much your manuscript has improved since you filed the old version away. More often than not you'll find your instincts were correct in the editing choices you made. Realizing this is gratifying, but more than that, it can give you the confidence to get past that sticky paralysis the next time you need to hack away at a draft.

12. USE A GUINEA PIG

If you're stuck revising and you can't bring yourself to make the cuts and changes that need to be made, it can help if you find a guinea pig: someone whose work you can practice on. It's easy to find another writer who wants a critique, or a writer who is willing to give you a copy of a rough draft to play with even if they don't want feedback. If you don't know other writers, sign on to Amazon.com, download some free novels, and practice on those.

Robert Spiller, author of the Bonnie Pinkwater mystery series, says that critiquing other people's writing always helps him get into the right mindset for revising his own work. Not only does he do this with the submissions from his regular critique group, he also volunteers his time as a judge for writing contests. This is a win-win scenario—he's sharing his writing expertise with others, while at the same time honing his own skills.

"Max" is a fantasy novelist who has also honed her skills judging for writing contests, but where she's learned the most is from analyzing published fiction. She dissected and analyzed dozens upon dozens of classics and bestsellers, learning which structures work, how "goal, motivation and conflict" looks in action, and a host of tricks, techniques and strategies. But Max's real lessons began when she started downloading free ebooks:

> Of the literally hundreds of free self-published ebooks that I read, only two were any good, and those went on to be picked up by "Big 5" publishers. The rest were varying degrees of awful, with most stories only starting three or four chapters into the book. I learned what a cardboard character really looks like, and saw first-hand how a series of events is not the same as a plot. This was truly the most instructional thing I've done to learn how to edit, and this knowledge has helped me get unstuck numerous times when doing revisions on my own work.

When you're making edits to another person's work, pay attention to what you do, then write down detailed directions as if you were instructing a novice how to edit. When you go back to your own work, if you are still stuck, following your own instructions can often get you past any reluctance to make the difficult cuts.

13. STEP AWAY

Step away from the manuscript. Take a giant step back.

Sometimes to get unstuck it's necessary to put some distance between you and your story. How much distance? How far do you go and how long do you stay away? It depends.

Award-winning fantasy writer Laura Resnick shares a specific method for a "5-10 minute reset" she learned from writing coach April Kihlstrom:

> I start typing (something! anything!) on the book ...and every time I freeze up or can't think of what comes next, I "reset" by getting up and doing something else for 5-10 minutes. (The timeframe is important. Prune a house plant; don't mow the lawn.) Then I come back after 5-10 minutes, sit down, and start typing again. During difficult phases, I've had days where I had to get up every 150 words ...but by the end of a day like that, I've written 1500 words. (My plants are also extremely well pruned at the end of such a day.) The point of leaving the desk as soon as I go blank, "resetting" with another activity, and then coming back and

> typing again is that it helps establish a repetitive behavioral pattern of being productive at my keyboard, rather than my keyboard being a place where I develop a habit of staring blankly at the screen until I give up.
>
> — Laura Resnick, *Misfortune Cookie: An Esther Diamond Novel*

Editor Tiffany Yates Martin of FoxPrint Editorial says that her number one piece of advice for writers when they're stuck is to get away from the story:

> I liken it to trying to build a house from the inside. You can do that for a while, but at some point you aren't seeing everything you need to see anymore. You have to step outside to check the structure, how it holds together, before you can go back in and know what needs to be built next. The way to get that objectivity, short of bringing in an objective reader, is to get your brain out of that world for a while—distract yourself, almost, so your creative mind takes a step back, out of the maze, and "reboots."

Author Elisa Lorello offers her techniques for gaining the type of objectivity Martin's talking about:

> Long walks, long drives, long showers. Not all at once, and not in any particular order. I also find that sometimes watching a particular film or television show, reading someone else's writing, or listening to a piece of music will help as well. Depends on the level/severity of

"stuck" and the subject/genre of writing (fiction, memoir, academic, etc.).

Horror writer "Gusto" Dave Jackson prefers distractions of the social variety:

> Dive into social activities, the wilder the better. In other words, don't hang around with homebody writers. There's nothing like some cutting-edge interaction to make you want to recreate the world.

Multi-published paranormal fiction author Lynda Hilburn has this to say:

> The primary way I get unstuck is to step away from writing for a couple of days and clear the mind. I like to take a walk, dance, sing, watch a funny movie or TV show. And of course, I sometimes get together with friends and drink wine.

Unfortunately sometimes it's necessary to step away from your writing for more than just an hour, an evening, a day, or a week.

Recently I spoke with "Kate" who's been stuck for several months on a young adult manuscript. She's tried lots of tricks and exercises to get unstuck, but nothing has worked, so we sat down for a long talk to try to get to the root of the problem.

After much discussion and some soul-searching on Kate's part, we discovered the "cause" of her block: her story is rife with teen angst and tragedy, which makes

Kate uncomfortable because she has a teenage son at home. While her son is happy, well-adjusted, doing great in school, and is nothing like the teens in her novel, it still makes Kate anxious to write the story. It's a lot more complex than that, but that's the gist of it.

To compound matters, Kate feels "very close" to completing this manuscript. She's on the tail end of her third revision, with the end being just out of reach. Her inner timekeeper is on her case to complete the book, right alongside the "goals police." These constant companions are relentless, and the more they push, cajole, and harass Kate, the more paralyzed Kate becomes.

She sits down to write every day, does not make any progress, and feels more like a failure with each week that passes.

When I first suggested to Kate that she consider stepping away from the project, she was torn. Part of her agreed that it was probably necessary in order to gain some perspective and objectivity, while another part of her didn't want to be a quitter and abandon her project. Eventually she came to see that stepping away is not the same as quitting. She would not be abandoning her project, just setting it aside.

What finally helped Kate decide to step away from the novel was making a specific agreement with herself: she made a list of ten short writing projects she wanted to do, and promised herself that upon the completion of each she'd "check in" with herself to see if she felt ready to return to her novel.

One short week after making this decision, Kate sent me this progress report:

> There's such a freedom in giving myself the opportunity to write about non-novel things without limit. I've realized how much I was depriving my inner writer. I'd take notes of all kinds of things that came to mind (like most writers do), but I told myself that I had to work on the novel first, finish it, and only then could I explore other things. I didn't realize how neglectful that was to my inner writer and ultimately hurting the novel too. I think the thing that resonates with me most—the thing I hope I never forget—is when you told me that no time spent writing is wasted; I have the knowledge, skills, and experience I gained when writing that novel, no matter what happens next.

I don't know if Kate will return to her young adult novel or not, but the bottom line is that she's writing.

A final word of caution: if you step away from a project, beware of stepping away *from writing* for too long.

> Knowing the human tendency for procrastination, I wouldn't recommend staying away for a long stretch of time. It seems as if that would just encourage you to accept writer's block as a way of life.
> — Stephen W. Saffel DEO,
> Senior Acquisitions Editor, Titan Books
>
> (DEO stands for Dark Editorial Overlord, a title given to him by one of his authors.)

My advice is, if you find it beneficial or necessary to step away from a project, resist the urge to stay away from writing altogether. Feed your inner writer and work on another writing project where you can feel successful and be reminded of the joy of writing.

PART THREE:
CHARACTER JUICE

> We sometimes encounter self-imposed speed bumps along the path to the final page. The key to overcoming those obstacles, I think, is to relax and let your characters tell their story. After all, the tale is about them, not you.
>
> — Lee Lofland,
> *Police Procedure and Investigation,*
> *A Guide For Writers*

Some writers seem to believe that their characters communicate with them. Are you of the mind that you "channel" your characters as if they are spirits with minds of their own? Or do you think that's a bunch of hooey? Either way, *acting as if* your characters can tell you their hopes, dreams, fears, histories, and the solutions to their own story problems is a process that can get you unstuck. Therefore some of the exercises in this section ask you to consult your characters. Whatever your beliefs, I encourage you to play along.

All the exercises in this section pertain to "character" in one way or another. It's probably pretty obvious that you'd turn to this section if you're blocked when it comes to a character, or if you can't seem to figure out what a character would do given your story situation. It may not be as obvious to try a character exercise when you're stuck on something like a turning point, and even less obvious if you're having difficulty getting words of any kind on the page. But these exercises can help then, too.

Why? Because characters drive the story. Just like characters are why *readers* care what happens next, the characters are also why *we as writers* care. Remembering why you love your hero or hate your villain can help you come up with that special something that turns the tables in the plot. Discovering a tidbit from a character's backstory can help you get excited about the story again. Immersing yourself in your character's world can inspire you to create stronger conflict. Learning what motivates your character can help you beef up the tension in your sagging middle and get you to the other side.

Whatever you're stuck on—no matter the details, regardless of the cause—spending time with your characters can help you see beyond the block and get you moving forward again. So buckle in for some exercises designed to give those characters some juice, make your story juicier, and get you juiced about writing again.

14. CHAT UP YOUR CHARACTER

When you're stuck, why not have a chat with your characters? Who better to help you get unstuck than the very characters who got you into this mess? The idea isn't to ask them why you're stuck (though it can't hurt to give that a try, if you'd like). The idea is to ask them questions about the story and see what you learn from their answers.

Bret Wright conquers writer's block by having conversations with his characters. Sometimes he talks with his main character, other times the supporting cast. In one instance when he was writing the detective story, *Getting Nasty*, he hit a wall where he could not figure out how to reveal a clue in a way that seemed natural and organic. So he turned to Nate Jepson, the detective protagonist of the series:

"Okay, Dude," Bret said. "What are you doing? Why do you even exist if you can't find a magic clue?"

"I'm trying to solve this case, but I need a break here, Writer-man," Nate said.

"Then help me out. Tell me what you usually do."

"I'm a people watcher, that's what I do," Nate said. "I

look for things that are out of place, people who don't fit in. I blend and I watch. If you don't know that, what are you doing writing me?"

"I think I know what you mean," Bret said. "But tell me more about how you'd go about finding this particular clue."

"Well," Nate said, scratching his head. "I suppose I'd start by walking down the street and I'd notice..."

The conversation continued with Nate describing the specifics of the street scene. Bret took notes as Nate pointed out the things he'd see that were out of place and the other characters there who'd catch his attention. After a while Nate finally got around to telling Bret the way he'd ferret out the critical clue, and Bret's problem was solved. He was unstuck.

Deb Courtney employed a more formal interview technique when she got stuck at a critical juncture writing *Infinite Yellow Flowers*. This project began as a memoir, but Deb decided she wanted to reshape it as a novel. The main problem in making this transition was that Deb's own real life did not have all the makings of a commercially viable character arc in a work of fiction. She needed to find a way to differentiate her character's "life" from her own. So she asked her character a series of questions about pivotal childhood events:

- What was your most embarrassing moment?
- Tell me about the outfit your parents did not want you to leave the house in when you were a teenager.
- Who was the first person that broke your heart?

- What was your dream car and what did you end up driving?
- Who betrayed you first, and how old were you?
- Tell me about your first pet—what happened to him?
- Who was the first person you knew who died?

Through the answers to these questions, Deb was able to substantially differentiate the character in the story from her real self. She did allow some overlap to remain—she let the character keep her dark, curly hair because there are "unique difficulties that come with having hair like that," and Deb wanted her character to share those difficulties. But mostly Deb used this exercise to turn the "Deb character" in a memoir into a fully fleshed out fictional character in a story that's only vaguely autobiographical.

Many times the answers to our story questions—and the key to getting unstuck—can be found in our character's backstory.

> The events of our childhoods flavor the rest of our lives, and color our reactions to present day events. Knowing the odd, the traumatizing, even the esoteric, about a character's past, can help us create consistent, real emotional responses in our characters that enrich and ground our stories.
> — Deb Courtney, Courtney Literary

By interviewing or chatting with your characters, you can glean tons of information about their personalities, likes and dislikes, history, and moral compass. Knowing our characters better—especially knowing their backstories— almost always helps us get unstuck.

15. SHOW ME YOUR PROFILE

Creating character profiles is a common practice among writers. Many do it at the start of the novel-writing process as a way of getting to know their new characters. Whether you are a regular profiler or not, a character profile can provide a goldmine of insight and information that can help you get past any number of blocks.

Some writers custom-create their own character profile templates. I use a modified version of one created by author Laura Hayden. I particularly like her inclusion of a secondary character trait that contrasts with the dominant character trait. I also appreciate the well-roundedness of thinking about how your character sees himself, as well as how others see him, and how he portrays himself in interactions with others. And what character profile would be complete without noting the character's favorite "pig out" food? Laura has been kind enough to share her profile in Appendix B so you can look it over and try it for yourself.

Another resource comes highly recommended by romance writer MK Meredith—WriteWayPro novel-writing software. MK loves using the rich profile forms that are built into the character files in the program:

> These profiles help guide me in accurately depicting my characters' reactions to different situations, expressing motivations, finding their secret yearnings, and discovering the direction they want their lives to take. From something as small as a scar on a brow to more significant facts about fears, every detail helps me add a robust realism to my people. They demand to be expressed to their fullest, and I can only follow their lead. Sometimes I'm quite surprised!

MK profiles her characters in the early stages of story development, and refers back to these profiles often during the course of writing the novel. She finds them particularly helpful if she gets stuck:

> If I come to a point where every word seems to have to be pulled from me with great strength, I go back through the profiles and always find threads that I didn't see before. Details that tie the lives in my stories together and return the momentum I thought had been lost. I remember when I was writing *Malibu Secrets*, a *Malibu Sights* novel, I struggled to figure out a way for the softer side of my hero to be revealed to my heroine. I immediately went to my profiles and discovered that when my hero was alone, he talked out loud to his mother who had passed away. Little did he know my heroine was close by. I love that scene.

In addition to profiling, there are loads of tools on the Web, in bookstores, and in magazines for assessing personality traits. From a light-hearted quiz in a magazine to the in-depth Myers-Briggs Type Indicator psychometric questionnaire, there's something for everyone.

Multi-published author Jaxine Daniels enjoys using the nine Enneagram personality types to define and develop characters, but she'd never used this as a method to get unstuck because she says she never gets stuck creating characters. That is until now. Her current project, *Revive 1775* (written as Jax Hunter), is quite different from her previous novels because it's based on real people from history. There's only so much she can learn from historical records and resources, which leaves gaps in her understanding of characters' motivations. This is where Enneagram comes in.

> I've been able to learn little about my heroine, Lydia, except what I can extrapolate from the tragedies that happened around her and the fact that she waited for the love of her life for eight long years. I can assume strength of character, perhaps. Dedication. Loyalty. But that's not enough to write her. So I go to my Enneagram books. Of the nine personality types, I'm drawn to Six: The Questioner, the Trouble-shooter. Sixes are loyal and likable and caring—that fits with Lydia. But they are also controlling and judgmental and rigid, motivated by the need for security. This sounds too weak for the Lydia I see in my mind's eye, so I try Four: The Romantic, the Individualist. Fours crave intensity and

stimulation, as well as being close to birth and death, catastrophe and serious illness. Wait just a minute—that's not Lydia, that's Sam, the love of Lydia's life!

Now I have a foothold. I plunge ahead, reading that Fours are most often attracted to—wait for it—Sixes. Well heck, maybe Lydia is a Six. I go back and read that when a Six is in a major crisis, she usually overcomes self-doubt and anxiety. That sounds less weak than I previously thought. I think about the scene I was stuck on and I try to visualize Lydia in that crisis moment. I can see her now, being insecure on the inside, but rising to the occasion and overcoming her self-doubt. And now I'm no longer stuck.

– Jaxine Daniels, *A Hard Place to Find*

So when you get stuck, try creating or revisiting a personality assessment, quiz, or profile for your character. If that doesn't open a door, be on the lookout for a window.

16. GROW A FAMILY TREE

Whether you're just getting to know your character or she's as familiar as the back of your hand, creating her family tree can reveal lots of interesting details you never considered. Details that can get you unstuck.

Start by tracing your character's lineage back a few generations, thinking about the connections between the relatives. Who did your character get her temper from? What about that crooked nose? Which relatives share his penchant for finding the gray areas of the law? Who bequeathed him the Rolex dive watch, and how did that relative come to possess it in the first place?

Think further about family lore, the stories passed down through the generations. How has family history shaped your character's perspective on the world? What does she view as "family traits;" which ones does she share and which does she wish she didn't have?

Creating a chart of family genealogy can be particularly useful and enlightening when writing in a fictional universe, alternate history, or futuristic setting.

The process of creating family trees is extremely useful in fantasy genres where the writer creates all history and lore. In *A Charm for Draius*, I started with a female protagonist in a matriarchal society, in which the matriarchy selects the male monarch and arranges all marriages. I barely had more than my protagonist's name and the idea she was "of the King's bloodline." By creating a family tree, I nailed down not only how she was related to the King, but the expected life span of her race, how matriarchs pass on their power and responsibilities, when a cataclysmic magical event occurred, what a recent plague did to her family, and why everyone within one generation calls each other "cousin."

– Laura E. Reeve,
the Major Ariane Kedros Novels

For me, when writing my post-apocalyptic *Seeds*, I needed to figure out how few survivors I could have in a closed community for that population to still be viable fifty years later. I created family trees for several characters and looked at how they were related. Once when I was stuck on a particular scene, I glanced back at the family trees even though the scene had nothing to do with family history. I noted that with each decade more and more of the population would be related, and it would be increasingly difficult to find unrelated "mates." This sparked an idea for a system of arranged marriage that not only got me unstuck in that scene but became an integral part of the plot.

No matter what you're stuck on, creating a family tree can be a fun way to come at the problem sideways, and it's sure to bring new facets of your characters to light.

17. WWYCD?
(WHAT WOULD YOUR CHARACTER DO?)

> My Dad, Tony Hillerman, didn't believe in writer's block. However, he admitted that he would sometimes "get stuck" in a novel. When that happened, he and Mom would get into their little pickup and drive out to whatever part of the Navajo Reservation he was using as a setting. The trip inevitably shook free the writing clog and got him back to work.
>
> – Anne Hillerman,
> *Spider Woman's Daughter*

When you get stuck, try doing something your character would do, eating something they'd eat, going somewhere they'd go.

Let's say you visit the zoo. While you're there, try to experience it from your character's perspective. Use all your senses: what do you smell, hear, and taste? What choices are there to make? Do you turn right to see the hippos or left to see the lemurs? Would your character's choice be different from yours? What would she be thinking as she passed through this space and time? How would the environment and the experience make her feel emotionally? Physically? Spiritually? What memories does it conjure? What longings come to mind? What regrets?

Robert Liparulo, author of the bestselling young adult series *Dreamhouse Kings,* takes this exercise one step further and recommends doing something *as* your character. He says, "To know your characters, be your characters." Go to a restaurant, park, church, strip club—wherever—*as your character*. Dress like her, talk like her, try to think like her. Note how people react and interact with the character—how is it different than how they'd relate to you? This process can open your eyes to all sorts of plot and character development options. So when you're stuck, spend a little time physically walking in your character's shoes (even if they're high heels, and yes, Robert did that!).

When Mandy Houk got stuck writing *Hope Is the Thing With Feathers*, she gave this method a try. After writing a couple of "really bad paragraphs and lame dialog" in a scene between the protagonist and his mother, she realized she wasn't making progress because she didn't know one of the characters well enough.

> I knew next to nothing about how Mother thought, what she felt about being left by her husband, why she'd even married him in the first place since he was kind of a prig. I had no idea what was going on in her head, what kinds of things she said to herself. So I opened a new document and wrote a diary entry in her voice. She ranted and cussed about her miserable life and how things had seemed so different when she'd first met her husband.

> How he'd sweet-talked her and fooled her, and now she was living with the consequences. She felt completely stuck with her kids who didn't seem to care about her feelings at all.
>
> She was a ball of rage, but she wasn't showing it outwardly, so I'd had no idea she was that angry until I journaled in her voice. This insight allowed me to understand that she'd be snippy and nitpicky with her kids on an almost constant basis. She'd be selfish, since she was so resentful of her lot in life. She'd be incapable of really loving anyone, because she was so set on receiving love, and so ticked about not getting it on her terms. All of that came through because I let her talk to herself in the journal—the only time she was ever really honest with me.

Mandy says that, though the journal entry didn't make it into the novel, it did get her unstuck in that scene. It also led to her decision to include chapters from Mother's perspective in the book so readers could hear her internal dialog and how it conflicted with her actions, making it a stronger story overall.

To do something as your character, you don't have to spend a lot of time, money, or effort. You don't even necessarily have to go anywhere. Just take a look at the activities in your normal daily life and think about which of these you could experience from the perspective of your character. Even if your story world is nothing like your own world, there will still be some common ground: eating, sleeping, showering, having an argument, doing the dishes, interacting with a pet, getting dressed. Find that common ground and see the experience through your character's eyes. This new perspective might help you get unstuck.

18. CONSULT A FORTUNE TELLER

How about a quirky, fun, quick way to get unstuck? Use one of the many readily available resources to "divine" what to do next in your story.

Try reading your character's horoscope in a newspaper or magazine. Is he going to meet a mysterious stranger who has a hidden agenda? Or come into unexpected money? Is a break-up or job loss or death of a loved one in his future? Mull over this information to see if it sparks an idea that moves your story forward. These horoscopes are typically written so broadly, there's bound to be an interpretation that will work for your story in some way. If it doesn't, try writing a scene where your character reads his horoscope. What are his reactions to it?

Fiction writer Tamsyn Coulon uses horoscopes in a more complex way when she gets stuck. For example, in her current manuscript she was unable to make progress because her character's reactions and opinions were wildly inconsistent. Tamsyn couldn't figure out what Liana would do in any given situation, much less what she would do next in the plot. So Tamsyn selected Liana's birth date, birth time, and exact birth place, then used a Western zodiac natal chart to discover the character's core nature. The results showed Tamsyn how Liana communicates with others, her career path, her relationships with her parents, her talents, fears, wounds, and issues. From this overall personality sketch, Tamsyn was able to create a comprehensive and consistent picture of Liana, and from there determine how she would act and react going forward in the plot.

Another horoscope option is to study the Eastern zodiac. You can use the personality portrait indicated by the character's birth year—year of the Horse, year of the Rabbit, year of the Snake, etc.—to ferret out a character's flaws, challenges, talents, and desires, all useful elements to think about when you're stuck.

The use of tarot cards can also be an excellent way to break through writing roadblocks. A good "spread" to try for character and story exploration is the Celtic Cross. This reading tells you who the character is at the present time in relation to a story question, what opposes or blesses them, what lessons they're learning, messages from their guides/mentors, their subconscious issues or fears they may not be aware of, what critical elements from their past are feeding into their current situation, what challenges they're currently facing, and the path they are taking through the story problem. Any one of those elements could speak to a turning point in your plot or character arc, and provide the fuel that propels your story forward.

When I was drafting *The Spider Prophet*, an alternate-reality fantasy with elements of Native American mythology, I knew I wanted the story to be a quest, but I was stuck on what tasks the protagonist should face during her journey. So I brainstormed the plot using a deck of "Medicine Cards" and their accompanying book *Medicine Cards: the Discovery of Power Through the Ways of Animals* by Jamie Sams and David Carson. By drawing a selection of cards and laying them out in a "medicine wheel spread," I was able to plot the main points in my character's quest, using the animals on each card to help determine the characters and challenges my protagonist would face.

Now you might think that this particular method would not have worked as well if my story was about space aliens rather than Native American totems, but the Medicine Cards, like any tarot-type cards, are based on archetypes, universal issues, and truths fundamental to human existence, so I believe even this specialty deck has the potential to spark a breakthrough idea for any story in any genre. Besides, if you're stuck, what have you got to lose?

19. RETAIL THERAPY

When the going gets tough, the tough go shopping. So if you're stuck in your writing, simply put down the pen or close the computer and head to the store for some retail therapy.

Of course I don't really mean you should forget all about your characters, your story, and your writing dreams and deadlines to take a stroll down Rodeo Drive or Fifth Avenue and purchase some non-essentials for yourself as a way to reduce your stress. I'm suggesting something a whole lot more fun, and less expensive to boot: go shopping for items for your character.

The whole idea of "shopping" is rich with questions to ask yourself about your character. First take the concept of shopping: procuring material goods in exchange for money. Perhaps this description fits your world quite well: your character grabs a gallon of milk from the local mini-mart fridge, hands the clerk some cash, and walks out with her purchase. But your character might procure milk an entirely different way if she lived in the same town back in 1800, in a third-world nation today, or a post-apocalyptic Paris. Imagine the possibilities if your character lives on a different planet, on an alternate-reality Earth, in another dimension, or in a fantasy realm completely unrelated to our galaxy.

Now think about your story and your characters: how would someone in your world procure goods he wants or needs? Think about the elements of the setting, the culture, the characters' economic standings, the availability of goods, the characters' access to those goods. Consider how "trade" works: is there currency, are goods traded, or both? Are there social taboos or customs governing who can trade with whom?

Give some thought to what types of things your protagonist and antagonist want or need to procure, what's at stake if they do not procure them, and to what length and expense they are willing to go to get them.

You can play this game even if your story is set in modern times and your characters are no different than the folks you rub elbows with in your real life every day. Even if shopping does not figure into your story at all, you can still ask yourself:

- What types of things would my character shop for?
- Does s/he like to shop?
- Would it be online or in person? Neiman Marcus or Wal-Mart or a thrift store?
- Would s/he spend more than s/he should?
- Would s/he buy more than the minimum necessities?
- What style of clothing or home furnishings would s/he like?

- Would s/he buy exactly what s/he likes, or would s/he select something "lesser" because of budget constraints, or something more ostentatious to try to impress someone?

When you're stuck, ask yourself these questions and more, then go shopping as if you were your character. You don't actually have to purchase anything, but try to look at the process through his or her eyes, thinking about the challenges s/he would face and the choices s/he would make. And though it's not required *per se*, I believe selecting his or her favorite outfit is a must.

20. *The Dream Vacation*

Where a person chooses to spend her leisure time and money can reveal a lot about her. Likewise you can learn a lot about a character by figuring out what her dream—or ordinary—vacation would be. So plan a vacation for your character. Protagonist, antagonist, secondary character—whoever you'd like to learn more about, or whoever it would be the most fun to plan for.

Do some sightseeing on the Web. Browse travel books from the library. Visit a travel agent pretending to be your character. Plan the vacation as if you were going, then write a scene that occurs at that locale. If it doesn't work for your current storyline, can it be backstory? If you want to immerse yourself in the exercise, create a collage with photos and magazine clippings of the vacation setting so you have a visual palette for your scene.

When Jade Goodnough was working on her post-apocalyptic dystopian *My Heart's End* she needed to provide her character Arabella with a reason to frequent a particular hot spring. This spring was the only place to bathe that was safe from animal predators, but this did not seem like a strong enough motivation for Arabella to keep returning there when each visit exposed her to the grave risk of discovery by nearby humans. Jade was stuck. The plot dictated that Arabella continue returning to the spring, but Jade couldn't figure out why she'd choose to do so.

Jade decided to try this exercise even though the story, the character, and the "problem" had nothing to do with going on vacation, and despite the fact that the concept of a vacation had little relevance in her post-apocalyptic landscape.

After brainstorming and surfing the Web for vacation spots, Jade landed on a locale that inspired her to create a backstory scene: Arabella and her husband were getting ready to take a dream vacation to a romantic, secluded resort with a hot spring high up in the mountains when the apocalypse took her husband's life. Since then Arabella's existence had been totally focused on surviving, and her hopes and dreams for romance and happiness were as dead as her soulmate. But the hot spring reminded her of the dream vacation she'd planned with her husband, and going there made her feel connected to him again. The desire to feel that connection gave Arabella a much stronger motivation to return to the spring.

With this realization, Jade was unstuck and on a roll again with a new backstory element that not only fueled Arabella's motivation in this scene, but began an entire new subplot.

The lesson: inspiration and insight can come from unlikely sources, so even if an exercise seems completely unrelated to your fictional world or your story problem, don't discount its potential to get you unstuck.

21. SEE DEATH IN YOUR FUTURE

If you knew you were going to die tomorrow, what would you do today? What regrets would you have about your life—things not said, not done, not lived? Would you try to remedy any of those? Would it be a quiet day? A wild day? A day spent in denial or disbelief? A day spent looking back, or a spent day living in the moment?

If you get stuck on any aspect of your story, take a "time out" to explore how your protagonist might spend his last day. What sorts of wishes and yearnings would he have? What choices would he make? What do these say about him as a person? If he had a reprieve, would he live his life any differently? Would he follow through with any of the things he wished he could do if he had more time?

When Jason P. Henry was stuck on his work-in-progress, he gave this exercise a try and learned that his protagonist, Dani Park, would spend her last day trying to help others achieve closure, something she had never been able to achieve for herself. He discovered that she'd try to connect with her parents who gave her up when she was five, which surprised him because he wouldn't make that choice himself.

In Jason's own words:

> When stuck, especially on a character, it helps to get inside their head. For a new character this is not always easy to do. The use of specific questions, like the ones in this exercise, forces you to play "situational improv." It narrows the scope of what you are trying to do and focuses your mind on specific traits instead of every aspect of a character's personality. For me, this exercise worked.

Ready to give it a try? Don't limit it to your protagonist. Give your antagonist a chance to reveal herself, too. Would she try to make amends on her last day? Would she be thinking of others? Would she regret her selfish, mean, destructive actions? Or would she wish she'd been better at being bad?

22. FISH OUT OF WATER

Open a book or magazine to a random picture, and imagine a situation that would cause your character to be there. Would this ever happen in your story? Why or why not? How could you incorporate a similar scenario in your story? Look at the event symbolically to see how a similar situation could become a scene for your protagonist or your antagonist. If it doesn't work for the body of your story, perhaps it could be backstory. Write a brief scene with your character in that setting and see where it goes.

When Julia S. Pierce was writing her middle grade fantasy novel *The Land of Yay* she got stuck at the half-way point—right at the dreaded "sagging middle" of the story. Her protagonist was flitting around, skirting the edges of the story, and Julia knew she needed to get her back into the action, but she didn't know how. Figuring she had nothing to lose, she decided to try this exercise.

The only printed material close at hand was a *Cooking Light* magazine. Even though Julia's story has nothing to do with food or cooking, she's a good sport so she opened to a random page. Staring back at her was a photograph of homemade marshmallows and orange-pecan tea bread.

Her first thought was "bakery," and though her stomach growled, it didn't provide inspiration in the context of her story. Then she thought "candy store." Nope, nothing there. Then "ice cream store." Hmmm. A pattern. A bunch of retail shops...From there it was a short leap to "cheap, touristy souvenir shop," and she had her answer.

Julia's protagonist had previously wrecked a sailboat that didn't belong to her, so Julia decided the character should get a job to pay for the repairs—here's where the bakery, candy store, and ice cream shop come in. Getting hired isn't easy for a twelve-year-old, and all these shops turn her down. Now she's slumped against the wall of the very last place she can apply: the souvenir shop. As she's trying to muster the courage to go inside, her "frenemies" show up to torment her. Ah, the frenemies! The backbone of this middle grade story!

An hour later Julia had cranked out 2,000 words that shored up that sagging middle with some conflict and tension. And all because of a cooking magazine and a photo of marshmallows and tea bread.

Cheryl Reifsnyder (aka Cheryl Reif) is so widely published in short fiction and nonfiction, I didn't think she ever got stuck. But recently she told me she was stalled crafting a young adult novel. She thought her character felt "flat," so she agreed to try this exercise to learn more about him.

Instead of opening a book or magazine for this exercise, Cheryl latched onto the image on her coffee mug: a bicyclist on the Mickelson Trail in South Dakota. Cheryl is familiar with this old Burlington Railroad route that's been converted for bicycle use, and it made her recall Deadwood, a small town along the route.

She plunked her character down in Deadwood and started asking questions: Why was he there? What would he do there?

But instead of going down the path of how the character would react if he visited this location, Cheryl's brain turned the scenario sideways and she found herself contemplating what it would mean if this character was *from* that location.

> What if my computer whiz kid was from a tiny town in the middle-of-nowhere South Dakota? Suddenly I started hearing his voice differently. I understood a strong motivation to spend a lot of time online while growing up (which I knew he had, but I hadn't considered why). I started imagining a friendship in his backstory, which may not play into the book itself but definitely gave me insight into his character.
>
> This wasn't at all what I would have chosen for my character's home town, but it fits perfectly. The "Fish out of Water" exercise helped in a completely unanticipated way...which is the way creative inspiration usually works, right?
> – Cheryl M. Reifsnyder, Ph.D.
> freelance science and medical writer

23. NICK A NAME

Hasn't everyone had a nickname at one time or another? Why shouldn't your character? If you're feeling stuck or stalled or simply uninspired, take a detour and explore this side road for a few minutes.

A fun way to come up with a nickname is to use a *random name generator*. Type "random name generator" into your search engine, and tons will pop up. Explore the possibilities (you may want to set a time limit or you could be entertained for hours). If the Web isn't your thing, try the phone book or cemetery headstones or sports team rosters for possibilities.

Once you've selected a nickname for your character, ask yourself these questions:

- Who uses the nickname?

- How did it come about?

- Does your character like it?

- Does your character think of him/herself that way (internal name)?

- What kind of image does the name portray? Is that appropriate to the character? To the genre? To the story?

- Does your character think the name "fits" him/her?

- Is this nickname different from one s/he would choose for him/herself?

When Susan Mitchell was stalled on her novel *Sangre*, she took a break from banging her head against the keyboard to give her character, Abuelita Belinda, a nickname.

She chose "Vieja" which means "old lady" in Spanish. Belinda's granddaughter uses this nickname to remind Belinda to behave as she should, like the old lady of the family. Like a grandmother, a matriarch, a respectable role model.

Belinda, however, thinks of herself as "forever young," youthful and sexy, and prefers to behave as such. She thinks she's far from old and has "plenty of good man-eating years" ahead of her. She hates this nickname.

Susan says that this nickname is not simply a stab in the back for Belinda, it's more like sinking a sword to the hilt and then twisting it, because getting old is Belinda's greatest fear. She's terrified that the name will fit her, which would signify losing her sex appeal, relinquishing her power, and thus being stripped of the tools that make life worth living.

> It's fabulous how the evolution of a nickname can inject a new level of depth into a character's personality and her relationships.
> – Susan Mitchell, *Sangre*

This exercise gave Susan insight into Belinda's character she hadn't considered before. It also gave her an idea for a scene that will dive into the psyche, history, and conflict of two main characters. And she's off to the races, no longer banging her head against the keyboard.

24. *ACCESSORIZE*

Sometimes we're so focused on the big, important things about a character that we neglect to develop other aspects. Like we make sure our character is wearing a shirt, pants, and shoes before leaving the house, but we don't note the accessories: the fabric of their sweater, the earrings they have on, if their socks match.

It may not be important what color underpants your character is wearing, or at least not important enough to include in a character sketch, much less in a chapter. But think about this character: an active duty army captain who wears tie-dyed boxers under his uniform. If you discovered this about your character, wouldn't it change the way you thought about him? This could open up all sorts of possibilities for getting unstuck, even if the underpants ultimately stay off the page.

When I suggest "accessorizing" your character, however, I don't actually mean with underwear and other garments. Instead I suggest adorning them with a hobby or other pastime, a sport or game, a quirk, a phobia, an addiction, a weird habit or unusual skill, even a pet.

If you look closely, you'll find examples in popular fiction: Robert B. Parker's Spenser is an ex-boxer; Nero Wolfe raises orchids; Indiana Jones is famously afraid of snakes; Elvis Cole has a feral cat and Stephanie Plum a pet hamster; and several of Jeffery Deaver's antagonists have hobbies—a watchmaker in *The Cold Moon*, a bug collector in *The Empty Chair*, and a cook in *The Kill Room*.

These accessories sometimes have bearing on the plot, but mostly they're in the background providing texture, complexity, humor, humanity. So if an accessory is mere "backdrop," why create one for your character when you're stuck? I think author Todd Mitchell says it well:

> I often like to remind myself that you can see more stars if you don't look directly at them. There's a physiological reason for this—something to do with there being more low-light receptors off to the sides of your eyes—but it's a good metaphor for writing. For me, it means that it's sometimes best to focus on the characters in the background, or seemingly off-center details and actions. Doing so can lead to surprises that bring the main character or story into focus. It's also a good way to get unstuck. Letting your mind drift off-center allows you to make unexpected discoveries that, more often than not, give light to the darkness.
>
> – Todd Mitchell, *Backwards*

So choose an accessory for your character. Go ahead and do it now—I'll wait. Be bold. Don't be afraid to make a choice. This isn't something you can get wrong. If you choose something that ends up not working, forget it and try again.

Once you've made your choice of accessory, think about how the character came to be involved in that particular activity, and create a brief backstory timeline from the first time s/he participated until present (or when s/he stopped). Then ask yourself what the emotional, financial, legal, relational, psychological, spiritual, and physical ramifications of this activity might be. Even if this activity is not a big part of the character's life in the present story, what residual evidence is there? How has it shaped him/her?

Still stuck? Write a scene pertaining to your character's accessory, and see if that shakes things loose. But don't look too closely at it or you might miss the star that lights your way out of the darkness.

25. TRAUMATIZE

Whenever author Darby Karchut gets stuck, she has a character fall off a cliff:

> Not one high enough to kill him or her. Just high enough to cause a problem. It is in the solving of *that* problem that I seem to be able to move the story along.
> – Darby Karchut, *Gideon's Spear*

I'd never thought about trying that, but I might now! What I usually recommend is to create a traumatic event in the character's *backstory*.

As real human beings, "who we are" is the result of all the things that have happened to us in our lives. Of course we're affected by good events as well as bad, but it's often the traumas that come to mind when thinking about things in our past that shaped us.

For example, I like the mountains. Why? I guess because they're pretty and I had some happy experiences going up to the mountains when I was a kid. But I can't recall a specific positive event that led to my liking the mountains. Likewise I can't tell you an event in my past that led to my current fondness for doing volunteer work. But I can tell you that I have a breed-specific fear of German Shepherds that's a direct result of being viciously attacked by one when I was ten years old. That childhood event shaped me. I still carry the scars—both physical and emotional—from a single incident that occurred decades ago.

I'm betting that tales of trauma from your own past have popped into your head now: a car accident, getting lost, being bullied, a pet dying, a parent dying, moving to a new town, your first broken heart. Sometimes it's obvious how these events have shaped us, but sometimes it takes some psychological excavation and puzzle-piecing to figure out how these events made us who we are today.

Why not give your character a traumatic event or three in his past that contribute to the "person" he is today?

If you like, when selecting this past trauma, you can target a trait that exists in your "page one character" and create a backstory event that would lead to that trait. For example, if my character is selfish on page one of my story, I can account for this with a backstory trauma like losing everything in a fire. Then it would make sense that she doesn't want to share things or give them away now—she's afraid of ending up with nothing again.

Or you can pick a backstory trauma without any thought to the result you want to produce. When you have this trauma in mind, think about the effects of that event over time, and how these "scars" would manifest in your page one character.

A great example of a character scarred by an event in his backstory is Jeffery Deaver's series protagonist, Lincoln Rhyme. When readers first meet Rhyme he's already a quadriplegic, and the *internal* scars from his backstory trauma are arguably deeper than his external ones. The reader doesn't need to know the details of the backstory event to appreciate Rhyme as a complex, intriguing character, but the character is undoubtedly stronger and more interesting because Deaver created that backstory.

I'm not suggesting you give your character a crushing blow that leaves him paralyzed, but definitely don't hold back when doling out the trauma. Give your characters a history rich with heartbreak and angst and tragedy, the worse the better. I'm not talking mundane stuff. Make it really bad. Losing a limb, losing a whole family, being the sole survivor of a village that was slaughtered, being buried alive, being stranded on a boat with a tiger...Oh wait, that's been done, but you get the idea.

These are the gifts that keep on giving, so be generous with the trauma. When you come back to your present-day story, your character and your story will be better for it, and chances are you won't be stuck any more. If you are, try adding another backstory trauma. Or have your character fall off a cliff. Stranger things have worked.

26. *EULOGIZE*

You know what they say—to get to know your character better, kill him off.

Wait, that's not a saying? Well it should be because writing your character's eulogy is a great way to get to know him better, and potentially a great way to get unstuck.

For this exercise, you're going to write a eulogy for your now-dead protagonist from the perspective of another character in your story. Think carefully about who would write the eulogy. It's how *this* character perceives and portrays your protagonist that we're focusing on right now, not how your character feels about himself.

A eulogy paints the dead as "larger than life." It's rare that anything negative is shared, and the positive things are often conveyed in the best possible light. What were your character's greatest accomplishments? What legacy did he leave? Make your character and his past actions shine more brightly than they actually did. Make others wish they could be that character. Make him a hero.

Since not everything in the eulogy must be "true," consider which parts would be accurate, which would be wishful thinking, and which outright lies. Think about how the eulogist might exaggerate or use revisionist history to color your character's actions as more noble than they actually were.

Think about what would *not* be said. What subjects would be vaguely referenced, avoided, or omitted, and why?

Some peripheral things that can be enlightening to consider:

- Where would the funeral be? What type of funeral? Would your character have left instructions or would the decisions be left to someone else (who)? Would anyone sing, and if so, which songs? Who would attend? How many people would actually miss your character? Who would be glad your character was gone?

- Would there be a burial, entombment, or cremation? Are your character's remains laid to rest near those of ancestors/family members/loved ones? What kind of marker would the resting place have—ornate, simple, modest, non-existent? Will anyone pay attention to this resting place after the funeral? Who and why or why not?

- Would there be a reception after the funeral? If so, who would host it and who would attend? Lots of people or few? Would it be solemn, or jolly in a bitter-sweet way? If alcohol would be served, who would drink too much and why? If no alcohol, why?

Would there be music? Would people be discussing their feelings and reminiscing about the deceased, or would they be holding their thoughts and feelings inside?

All of the above looks at your character from the outside. It can also be useful to see this from inside your character. Think about the funeral from your character's perspective, as if he were witnessing it from the grave:

- How would he feel about the eulogy? What would he like and what would he hate? What would he wish he could speak to, to set right? What are his thoughts about the person who delivered the eulogy?

- What would he think of the service? Which funeral attendee would be the biggest surprise? Who is conspicuously absent, and was their absence expected?

- What would your character say he would miss the most about life? What regrets would he have? If he could go back and change just one decision in his life, what would it be?

Rachael Dahl was stuck on a work-in-progress because she is "too protective" of her characters. She doesn't want to air their dirty laundry or emotions, so she leaves those internals out of the story. The result is that Rachael can't connect with her characters. They fall flat, and the story stalls.

To get unstuck, Rachael knew she needed to get in touch with her characters' emotions, and convey these emotions on the page. But this would mean tapping into her own emotions, which she prefers to keep locked inside. She didn't want to reopen the wounds of her own personal losses and relive that pain. So she remained stuck.

Eventually, however, Rachael's need to write the story prompted her to take another try at getting unstuck. She chose to directly confront her own pain at having recently lost four family members by doing this eulogy exercise.

> When my story begins, my protagonist, Ava, is starting college a semester late because her mother passed away a few months earlier from cancer. Right after her mom died, Ava had debated killing herself, even bought the gun, but couldn't go through with it. In her safe place where she stores her gun is a copy of her eulogy. She wrote it to spare her father the pain of having to do it, since writing his wife's eulogy emotionally and physically wrecked him. I didn't know all of this backstory until I did the exercise. I knew Ava had thought about suicide, but I didn't know she couldn't bear to put her father through the pain of writing her eulogy.
>
> Before I wrote Ava's eulogy, she was still a cardboard figure to me. A Flat Stanley. But now I can hear her, see her, even smell her soap. The worst part for me is that I can now feel her pain too. But it was necessary. I had to allow my own pain to come to the surface in order to write Ava's story properly. I'm ready to do that now, pain and all.
>
> – Rachael Dahl, *Shattered Lives*

If you're stuck, consider seeking a different perspective on your character, your story, and even on yourself, by killing off your protagonist and writing a eulogy. Don't worry—not everyone has to bleed onto the page like Rachael did to benefit from this exercise, but sometimes that's what it takes to get unstuck.

PART FOUR:
STORY MECHANICS

Do your story mechanics need a mechanic?

There are a lot of complex moving parts to a story. When they're all working properly and in harmony, you barely notice they're there.

Like a car. You turn it on and it comes alive, purring and whirring and humming as it should. You put it in gear and go, never thinking about the mechanisms at work...until something goes awry. Instead of a hum there's a *kachunk*, the purr becomes a grinding sound, the whirr a squeal. Now you're very aware of the mechanics and the fact that they're not working properly. Maybe something's a little out of whack, or maybe it's a serious break. Either way it must be repaired.

With your story, when you get stuck it might be a big *kachunk* that requires serious fixing, or a little squeal that simply needs grease. Either way, the exercises in this section can help get your story running smoothly again, so you can cruise along without any grinding noises to distract or concern you.

Ready? Set? Writers, start your engines.

27. PROGRAM YOUR GPS

One of the most important things we writers can ask ourselves is "Where is my story going?" After all, you can't figure out how to get there if you don't know where "there" is.

If you're stuck in your story journey, one of the best ways to get unstuck is to determine where the story will end: the destination.

Knowing what kind of writer you are to begin with will help you to understand the best destination method for getting unstuck:

- If you already know your destination, and in fact have planned exactly how to get there down to the last detail, then you're the type of writer we'll call "the Plotter."

- In the other camp are the writers who reject planning, who've come to believe that plotting easily turns to "plodding," where the magic and joy of discovery is lost. If you prefer to write "into the ether," stream-of-consciousness style, to write "by the seat of your pants," then you're what we'll call "the Pantser."

(I don't claim to have coined the terms "Plotter" and "Pantser," but I wish I had—they're quite useful.)

Plotters might be inclined to dismiss this exercise because you already know the destination of your story. It would be just as easy for Pantsers to reject it because it involves planning. But I have news for both Plotters and Pantsers: what you learn from the way the other camp operates in this exercise might be *your* key to getting unstuck.

Are you with me?

PANTSERS: this is for you. (Plotters are welcome to join us. I'll be preaching to your choir, but you're welcome to sing along.)

Pantsers, this may be hard to hear, so brace yourselves: I've conducted an informal survey of Pantsers over the past ten years, and have found that virtually every single successful Pantser knows the destination of their story. By "successful" I mean those who complete manuscripts (many of which sell), i.e. those who are not stuck.

Before you reject the notion of setting a destination, you should know that pretty much every Pantser I talked with rejected it at first, too.

"I don't have a plan," they'd say. "I just write."

But when I dug deeper, I found that they *did* have a destination in mind when they wrote. They simply did not recognize it as a "plan."

Take romance author Jodi Anderson (aka Jodi Dawson), for instance. She's pantsed her way through several successful novels "without a plan." But *with* a destination: the hero and the heroine are together in an emotionally satisfying relationship at the end. Both the hero and heroine must grow and change in order to "earn" that ending. That's her destination. That's her plan. She happily pantsed through the story without an outline, but she knew where she wanted to end up, and that helped her to eventually get there.

Think of it like going on a road trip. You don't have to use a map, or plan your stops, or figure out how long to spend in any one place. But if you start driving without knowing where you want to end up, how do you know which direction to go? North? South? And along the way, how do you know if you should turn east or west at the junction? You don't. This makes it easy to get stuck at a crossroads.

Author Michael Shepherd is a successful Pantser. He doesn't plan, he doesn't plot. His "outline" for a novel is nothing more than a scribbled paragraph. He lets the story play out as he writes. He says that his characters seem to know what needs to be done, and he's often surprised by their actions.

Did you catch that? His characters "seem to know what needs to be done." Hmmm. When I heard that, I thought it sounded like *his characters had a destination*...So I questioned Mike a little more.

"How do your characters know what to do?" I asked. "Do *they* have a destination in mind? An end-goal they're working toward?"

"Actually, they do," Mike said. "For example, in my novel *Hell With a Gun*, the entire story is based on one thought: 'How far would a father go to save his daughter?' So I suppose the father character had a 'destination,' if you want to call it that. To save his daughter."

"Ah," I said. "And does he save her?"

"I don't want to give away the ending," Mike said. "But *I* knew the answer to that question all along. That's what I was writing toward. In fact, I kept that phrase 'How far would a father go to save his daughter?' taped to my computer screen so that when I got stuck, it would remind me what I was trying to do. That one little phrase made me remember that my protagonist was the only one who fully understood how much he had to lose, that he'd have an escalation of awareness he was in a situation from which he couldn't extricate himself—a pit from which he could not escape—and the only reason to enter that pit was his belief that his daughter could be saved from it. So yeah...I guess I had a destination."

So, Pantsers, think about it: does your story have a destination, however vague? If you're stuck, try defining that destination for yourself. If looking at your end-goal doesn't get you unstuck, consider looking at the destination of the specific scene you're stuck on. I know it goes against your grain, but give it a try. This does not mean that suddenly you're a Plotter and you'll plan out every scene. It's just a technique—a trick, if you will—to get you over the hump, past the roadblock, and through the woods to Grandmother's house, or wherever your final destination may be.

PLOTTERS: this is for you.

Many Plotters swear that their planning keeps them from getting stuck:

> I honestly don't get stuck that often, mainly because I outline like a fiend. I write mysteries and I need to know whodunnit and whytheydunnit. Outlines save me from the mud. They also save me from writing in a straight line from beginning to end. It means I can write the middle before I write the beginning. Which is good because, you know, writing beginnings is scary.
>
> – Elspeth Futcher

But if you're reading this, I'm guessing you're stuck despite your planning, or at the very least you're concerned you might get stuck one day. Never fear, I have something that will help the plottingest of Plotters, but fair warning: you might not like it.

If a Plotter is stuck, it's likely for one of two reasons:

1. Not planning enough
2. Planning wrong

As for *not planning enough*, romantic suspense author Laura Kenner is a Plotter, and she finds that she gets stuck at places in the story that she glossed over during the planning process. The "...and stuff happens" part of the plot outline (which we all know is shorthand for "I'll figure it out when I get there") can often translate into writer's block.

The lesson here is to take your well-honed plotting skills and bring them to bear where you're stuck. What's the destination of that scene? It should in some way get you closer to or further from the end-goal (or final destination) of your book; otherwise you don't need the scene. Think about the milestones you want to hit in that scene—what do you need for your character to learn or accomplish? What clues do you need to reveal? What future event do you want to foreshadow? What past event do you need to allude to? What challenges do you want the character to face?

Perhaps more important than thinking about what *you-as-the-writer* want and need, think about what the point-of-view character in this scene wants and needs. What is his destination in the scene? Why? If you've defined his destination and are still stuck, it could be that you don't understand why *the character* wants to get there (even if you know why you-as-the-writer want him to get there). If you give him a clear reason for wanting to get to the destination, and a strong motivation to get there, you most likely won't be stuck any longer.

Yes, I'm asking you to do more planning. This you understand. This you like. This you can do. But what if all your brilliant planning still doesn't get you unstuck?

If this is the case, you probably planned *wrong*, by which I simply mean that you chose the wrong destination for your scene. If you chose wrong, no re-working of the currently plotted scene will help, and you need a new tactic: Pantsing. I warned you that you might not like it. I know it goes against your grain, but if you're stuck, don't you owe it to yourself to give it a try?

Here's what you do: disregard everything you had planned except for the end-goal (final destination) *of the story as a whole*. Yes, set aside the destination you had in mind for the scene. Don't argue, just do it. Now, put yourself in the mind of the point-of-view character of that scene. Assess where she is now versus where she wants to go ultimately. What is in her way? When she heads down her path, what's the first thing that blocks her? Now write a scene where she confronts that thing. Yes, write it without a plan. No one ever has to see this writing—it's just for you. So resist the urge to plan, and plunge in. Write the scene through to its natural conclusion.

How does the outcome of the new scene affect what comes next on your character's journey? Is she on a different path to the final destination than the one you originally plotted? Is it a *better* path? If you're not happy with this new course, repeat this free-write exercise until you get past the block and are happy with the results.

Try to be open to any solution, even it requires you to re-plot some—or all—of the story. After all, you're good at plotting. You know how to do that. Making a new plan is no problem—even fun—when you're no longer stuck.

Bonus technique to *stay* unstuck: plan *your* destination for the next time you write.

"Leigh" is an award-winning mystery and science fiction writer who unfortunately has a long-running bloody battle with writer's block. She's tried plotting, she's tried pantsing, but still she gets stuck. While she's not completely "cured" she has found one tactic that works better than anything else she's tried. It's what I'd call a hybrid plotting-pantsing compromise.

She says that, whether you're a Pantser or Plotter when it comes to *writing your story,* be a Planner for what you'll write in your very next scene.

> The most frightening thing for me about writing is the great unknown. If I don't know what I'm going to write about the next time I sit down, it's a sure-fire way to make sure I don't sit down at all. It's too scary. It's like setting off on a voyage over stormy seas without knowing what kind of boat you have, what provisions you need, or even how long you'll be at sea. There's no way I'd get in that boat.

To overcome this fear, at the end of each work period Leigh jots down some ideas about what she thinks will happen next in the story.

> It might be something related to plot, like "Make sure Joe follows up on Pam's veiled hint that she is seriously ill." Or it could be something that helps create atmosphere, such as "Have the TV on when Joe gets home, some charlatan touting his snake oil

supplement, and Pam is actually listening to the guy." These quick little bullet points are like a primer coat, preparing my subconscious to lay down the next event in the story (be it an action scene, a conversation, whatever). I think of it as water-proofing that boat so it doesn't sink before I even get started.

This small "plan" for what to write next gives Leigh the courage to face the blank screen.

Finally, the big moment arrives. The ship is ready to sail, and I'm ready to get on board. I sit down at my computer, and Joe verbally assaults Pam for her carelessness in not seeing a doctor, then she lashes into him for not caring...and my day's work is off and running. But without the tiny bit of prep I did the day before, I might not have made it to the boat at all.

28. GOT GMC?

GMC: Goal, Motivation, and Conflict by Debra Dixon describes a process for determining the goal, motivation, and conflict for each character in your story. Dixon recommends using this technique for the story overall *and* for each scene, addressing both the inner and the outer versions of GMC for each character.

If you haven't tried the GMC process, you'll be amazed how much it helps you understand your plot and your characters, which can help you get unstuck and stay that way.

If you're stuck and you've already done GMC for your story, it's time to look back and see if what you planned is still valid.

According to multi-published author and acclaimed pitch coach Linda Rohrbough, "The Big Mistake" that writers often make is not having a highly motivated character overcoming obstacles to achieve a goal. So if your story's not working, it could be because your character is not highly motivated, is not overcoming obstacles, and/or is not trying to achieve a goal.

Are you stuck because you had the "wrong" goal in mind for your character? Or because his motivation is too weak? Or because there's not enough conflict to provide him with a challenge? Or due to some other reason altogether? The way to find out is to do (or re-do) GMC for the scene you're stuck on. If that doesn't fix things, look at GMC for the overall storyline for each character. Chances are good you'll discover the problem that's hanging you up.

Here is my brief interpretation of Dixon's GMC process:

GOAL (G)

A goal is what a character wants. In commercial fiction the protagonist always has an external goal. If you want a multi-layered, complex character, you should also give him/her an internal goal. Goals should be important, urgent, specific, and attainable. The big central goal of a character is often accompanied by a series of smaller goals that drive the action of the story. Each scene should move a character closer to or further from a goal.

A character can have multiple goals simultaneously, and a character's goals can change over time. Goals can start small and change over the course of the novel. Keep in mind that readers like things to connect, so if a character's goal changes, it's nice if the new goal relates in some way to the old one. Dixon points out that internal goals often remain consistent while external goals change.

Some goals are achieved, some not. If the character's overall goal for the story is not achieved in the end, the story still needs to be satisfying to the reader.

MOTIVATION (M)

Motivation is *why* the character wants what s/he wants; it's why the character wants the goal. Dixon advises keeping it simple, strong, and focused. Readers will "buy" a character's decision if they accept the character's motivation. Think about the girl in the horror movie who goes into the dark basement alone. You might be inclined to say, "That's not realistic—I'd never do that," unless you know she's going down there to save her dog/sister/child.

Internal motivation is often psychological, like "to be loved" or "to be a success." It should be logical given the specifics of the character and story—think about the genre, as well as the character's age, gender, culture, etc. A good way to understand your character's internal motivation is to create a backstory that explains why your character is motivated in that way. For example, the motivation "to be accepted" could stem from a history of rejection.

CONFLICT (C)

Conflict is the thing that gets in the way of a character achieving his/her goal. It's the reason why the character can't have what s/he wants. It's what opposes him/her. You can think of external conflict as plot, and internal conflict as the character's arc.

A villain makes an excellent, well-defined external conflict for the hero, but don't neglect to give the villain his/her own GMC. It often works well when the hero is the "C" for the villain, and the villain is the "C" for the hero. If there's not an evil villain in your story, there should be someone who works at cross purposes to your hero. In a romance, the hero and heroine often work at cross purposes to each other.

Here's my take on protagonist Katniss Everdeen's external GMC in The *Hunger Games* by Suzanne Collins:

G: she wants to win the Hunger Games.
M: she wants to live (if she loses, she dies); also, winning provides a lifetime of food and money for her and her family.
C: she's weaker than most of the other tributes who are trying to kill her.

Ready to try it for your story? If you'd like a little practice first, try doing GMC for a familiar book or movie. You can start with Katniss' internal GMC in *The Hunger Games*, or perhaps for fun compare her external GMC from this book with her GMC in *Catching Fire.*

29. LINE UP

A "logline" is the essence of your story distilled to one short sentence that typically answers the question: "What is the story about?"

If you're stuck, creating such a logline can help you refine your thinking down to the most basic premise of your story, and get you back on track.

If you're stuck and you already have a logline, now is a good time to revisit it to see if you've strayed from your original story premise. If you have, decide if you want to revise the logline or revise the storyline. This process can often help you get unstuck.

To construct a standard logline, you need these three elements:

1. **Character**: who is your story about? Typically you want a description, not a name. I suggest using a "dominant impression" as described by Dwight Swain in *Techniques of the Selling Writer*: an adjective plus a noun of vocation (e.g. scatterbrained writer, neurotic housewife, murdering dentist).

2. **Goal**: what does your character want? This refers to the character's overarching goal in the story. This can be the internal goal or the external goal, or you can include both.

3. **Conflict**: what's keeping the character from getting the goal? This can also be internal and/or external.

You can also add a fourth element, what I call a "Plus"—a little something extra that adds nuance, texture, a sense of setting, and/or a "hook" that captures interest. I also like for it to evoke emotion so that I feel connected to my story when I read it.

Let's look at an example.

EXAMPLE LOGLINE:
A girl on a reality TV show has to make difficult ethical choices in order to win.

This is a very general logline. Too general. It might have the required elements, but it could be about any story, at any time, in any place. We know next to nothing about the character or the world. There's no hook. There's not enough detail or emotion for it to resonate with me as the writer.

I'll try to improve on that example.

IMPROVEMENT ATTEMPT #1:
In the future, amidst the ruins of North America lies the nation of Panem where a 16-year-old girl who is a loner and sole supporter of her family, Katniss Everdeen, takes her younger, weaker sister Prim's place in the

nationally televised Hunger Games where she's a longshot to survive the fight to the death against other teenagers from every District—a fight to the death on live TV.

Yes, this is a logline I created for *The Hunger Games* by Suzanne Collins. Did you realize when you read the *first* logline that it was also for *The Hunger Games*?

Looking at the "improved" version, it's certainly not too general any more, but I think it's too wordy with way too many clauses and details. It does convey more of the world and the character, but the density of the sentence makes it difficult to follow, and thus hard to connect with emotionally.

IMPROVEMENT ATTEMPT #2:
A desperate 16-year-old fights to be the sole survivor of the Hunger Games, but at what cost to her humanity?

I think I'm getting somewhere now. Here's how this version breaks down:

A desperate 16-year-old (CHARACTER) fights to be the sole survivor (EXTERNAL CONFLICT, GOAL) of the Hunger Games, but at what cost to her humanity? (INTERNAL CONFLICT)

I think we can agree this version is better, but I don't think it's as good as I can make it. I'll try adding the "Plus."

IMPROVEMENT ATTEMPT #3:
In what used to be North America, a desperate 16-year-old battles to be the sole survivor of the nationally televised "Hunger Games" where teens fight to the death, but at what cost to her humanity?

Here's the breakdown:

- *In what used to be North America (PLUS);*
- *a desperate 16-year-old (CHARACTER);*
- *battles to be the sole survivor (EXTERNAL CONFLICT, GOAL);*
- *of the nationally televised "Hunger Games" where teens fight to the death (PLUS);*
- *but at what cost to her humanity? (INTERNAL CONFLICT).*

This version works for me because it combines the elements necessary to understand the premise of the story, while at the same time evoking a world and character that resonate with me. In other words, I not only understand what the story is about, I feel connected to it. If I were writing *The Hunger Games*, I believe this logline would help me remember what story I'm trying to tell and why.

By forcing yourself to write a logline, you are making yourself identify and articulate the heart of your story. This in itself is a powerful tool for getting unstuck.

Once you have that logline, post it where you write to remind you what your story is about. If you get stuck because you've veered off course, the logline can help you get your bearings and regain your focus so you can move forward again.

30. THE HERO'S JOURNEY

I'd like to say that the Hero's Journey is my best-kept secret for writing successful fiction, but that would be a lie. The "secret" is a basic pattern found over centuries in narratives around the world. It's a structure so fundamental to fiction, it was embedded in my subconscious before I can remember—back when my dad told me bedtime stories before I could read—and cemented by the tales I grew up on: *The Wizard of Oz*, The Chronicles of Narnia, *Star Wars*, *The Lion King*, Harry Potter, *The Hunger Games*. (Okay, you caught me —I was already grown up for some of those.)

When I started crafting my own stories as a kid, I followed the Hero's Journey pattern without knowing that's what I was doing. Much later I became aware of it as a classic storytelling structure through Joseph Campbell's *The Hero with a Thousand Faces*, but I wasn't yet pursuing writing as a career, so it slipped into the recesses of my memory. Years later when I began writing fiction in earnest, I was reintroduced to the Hero's Journey by Christopher Vogler in *The Writer's Journey*. Vogler explains the structure in a clear, concise manner I find totally accessible (and a whole lot less academic than Campbell's work) as well as totally applicable to my own storytelling process.

After I read Vogler's book I began to see the Hero's Journey everywhere: *The Little Mermaid, The Notebook, Outlander, The Matrix, Die Hard, Mission Impossible, The Golden Compass.* At first my family hated when I'd blurt out during a movie, "That's the Call to Adventure." But now they join in the fun, shouting "Look, she's Crossing the First Threshold" or "He's Approaching the Inmost Cave" as often as I do.

I think a lot of writers reject using a structure like the Hero's Journey on the basis that it's formulaic or derivative, and I can relate to that. But the Hero's Journey structure is as pervasive and successful as it is because it resonates in some profound way with the human psyche, and I think we as writers can learn a lot from it whether we choose to follow it in our own writing or not. Know "the rules" (or the structures or the formulas) and then use them or not, it's up to you.

The Hero's Journey breaks down nicely into the "three act structure" commonly used in popular fiction. Here's my version of the basic components of the journey laid out in that three act structure. Note that not every story with this structure must include each of these elements or follow this precise order.

ACT ONE

The Ordinary World: the hero in his/her normal life, whatever that "normal" is.

The Call to Adventure: the hero has an opportunity to enter a new/special/different world.

The Refusal of the Call: the hero turns his/her back on the adventure, returning to the ordinary world.

The Mentor: the hero gains knowledge/supplies/confidence.

Crossing the First Threshold: the hero commits to the adventure, enters the special world.

ACT TWO

Tests, Allies, Enemies: the hero learns the rules of the special world, gains tools/skills/knowledge.

Approach the Inmost Cave: the hero prepares for the ordeal.

The Ordeal: the crisis, *not* the climax; this shows the reality of failure/death; the hero comes out changed/reborn.

Seize Sword of Victory/Reward: momentary celebration.

The Road Back: the rest of the journey; the hero recommits to the goal.

ACT THREE

The Resurrection: the climax; the last and most dangerous meeting with death.

Return with Elixir: the denouement; the hero returns to the ordinary world with something to change it, or starts a "new normal" as a changed person.

There are tons of resources where you can learn more about each of the components of the Hero's Journey and how they fit together, but you don't have to spend any more time on it than you want to. A basic understanding of the mythic structure and archetypes can give you options when you're stuck, stalled, or in the doldrums.

Novelist Anya Rakoczy had a long, rocky start to *The Right Hand of Darkness*. She spent several years writing and revising drafts of this paranormal romance, including crafting three alternate endings, but she never felt like the pieces of the puzzle were fitting together quite right. "It felt out of joint," she says. "Like there were some brilliant scenes, but they weren't in the correct order." She got stuck in a vicious cycle of revision that never seemed to fix the story.

Enter The Hero's Journey. Anya attended a writer's retreat where she workshopped her broken manuscript with a small group of experienced writers. The leader encouraged Anya to break down her story into the components of the Hero's Journey to see if that would shed any light on why she wasn't progressing. During this process, Anya got more than she bargained for.

Anya combed through her manuscript, placing key scenes into the Hero's Journey template. What she had when she was done shocked and amazed her. She realized that a huge reason the story wasn't working was because she hadn't written a paranormal romance at all, but had actually penned a more traditional hero's arc in an urban fantasy setting. Another reason the story wasn't working—and the ending in particular—was that the scene she thought was the climax was actually the "ordeal." Further, her story only had nine of the twelve components of the Hero's Journey, and adding the missing three (even though it's not required) filled some critical holes in the story that Anya hadn't seen before.

Since this great realization, Anya has changed her perspective on her story, embracing it as an urban fantasy battle between good and evil where the hero becomes a vampire and undergoes a dramatic arc, eventually making peace with his new normal and thriving. Though there is still a romantic subplot, recognizing that the story is not a paranormal romance enabled Anya to eliminate scenes and details that were detracting from the main storyline. This process as a whole enabled her to craft and pen an ending that feels right. "Without the Hero's Journey," Anya says, "I'd still be trying to fit an urban fantasy 'puzzle piece' into a paranormal romance 'hole.'"

So if you can't figure out what happens next in your story, or you're going round and round on revisions that never make the story exactly right, try consulting the history of storytelling to see which pattern your story follows and what "should" happen. You can then decide to follow the classic journey or depart from it in a conscious, purposeful way—either option should get you moving past your block.

31. GET ON THE GRID

A "plotting grid" is a physical chart used to lay out the components of a story in a visual way. Doing a Web search on the words *plot, grid,* and *fiction* should yield some useful examples.

The grid I use was introduced to me years ago by author Robin Perini, and consists of twenty squares laid out on a poster board in four rows of five. Each square represents a main plot point progressing in chronological order from the top left to the bottom right of the board, just as you'd read words on a page. The squares on the right-hand side of the board are turning points in the story.

An optional component on my board is a section to document the main characters' GMC (goal, motivation, and conflict, a concept made popular by Debra Dixon's book of the same name). I personally like to chart internal and external GMC for the protagonist and antagonist, as well as a third character (typically the love interest or secondary protagonist) for a total of three character GMCs on display to remind me where my story is going and why.

A visual story chart like a plotting grid can be useful at any stage of writing, but can be particularly helpful when you're stuck whether or not you typically plot your story in advance. Simply filling in the blanks with key story elements can give you a new perspective on your story that in itself can get you unstuck. If that doesn't do the trick, use the grid to help you delve into deeper analysis of your story structure and components to try to figure out what is "wrong." It can be particularly illuminating if you overlay the elements of a classic story structure (like the Hero's Journey) to help you identify elements that are missing or out of place in your story.

Fantasy author Mike Haspil is a recent convert to the plotting grid method, frequently foisting it on his critique partners and unsuspecting strangers, and singing its praises whenever he has the opportunity.

> When I start writing a novel, I don't have an extensive plan, but I usually have a firm story concept, a few key scenes in mind, and an idea for the ending. When I discovered the plotting grid, it seemed like the perfect tool to document these components—I could fill out the parts of the story I knew and put them approximately where I thought they would go in the overall plot. I tried this for a few works-in-progress and appreciated the results, so on my most recent novel, I filled out every element on the plotting grid before I started writing. Then I plunged into the first draft, never stopping to refer back to the grid, even though it was sitting in the same room. After all, I'd done the planning and I knew where my story was going.

I was pretty far along in the story when I found myself hopelessly stuck. After a day or two of banging my head against the keyboard, I turned to the plotting grid intending simply to identify a handful of scenes that I could write out of sequence until I got back on track. But checking the grid, I found that my story had gone wildly off the rails and that the pacing was entirely too slow. In my mind, I was just rounding the corner of Act I, but by my word count and number of scenes, I should have been well into Act II. I wound up cutting almost 20,000 words, my story bounced back on course, and I was no longer stuck. Now I consult the grid every time I get stalled, as well as giving it a periodic glance when I'm not stuck just to make sure my story stays on course.

– Michael F. Haspil, *Graveyard Shift*

32. CHECK YOUR PERSPECTIVE

When you're stuck it's a good idea to check your perspective. By this I don't mean to check your attitude or perspective on writing, or even your perspective on your story, though I suppose those couldn't hurt. What I'm referring to is the perspective *of* your story.

If your story is told in the first person, would it work better if told in third? If your story is all told from one character's point-of-view, what about telling it from the point-of-view of a different character? Or maybe try *adding* a perspective—an additional point-of-view character. If your story is told in past tense, how about telling it in present?

You can try any of these changes for the story as a whole, or you can try changing just the part you're stuck on. For example, if you are having difficulty writing a scene, swap to a different character's point-of-view and write the same scene from that perspective.

When Anne Eliot was writing her first book, *Almost, a Love Story*, she got terribly stuck trying to make her heroine relatable and likeable to the reader. She realized her protagonist came across as cold and mean because "her wound and subsequent mask was so deep and hidden readers could not find her." Anne tried changing the starting point of the story, she tried starting the story from a different character's perspective, she tried everything she could think of, but the main character remained inaccessible to the reader.

Anne was so frustrated, she quit writing altogether. But it's hard for a writer to not write, so it wasn't long before she went back at the manuscript with a new tactic: she changed the entire story from third person to first, and *voilà*! The reader could now see more clearly what was going on inside the protagonist, what caused her pain and fears, and why she was making the choices she made. By changing to a first person perspective, Anne made the character relatable and this made all the difference. Thank goodness Anne decided not to quit writing—*Almost* went on to land her the New York agent of her dreams, and became a top seller on Amazon, as well as being translated and sold abroad.

33. LIST IT

Are you a list maker? I am. I love listing all the things I need to get done on a project, and derive an inordinate amount of satisfaction from crossing things off the list. It's not my fault—this runs in my family. One of my sisters makes a list each day of the things she needs to get done, and it always includes "wake up" just so she has the pleasure of crossing it off.

When you've got a halting case of writer's block, making a list can be a valuable tool for getting unstuck, even for you non-list-makers out there. Multi-published author and ghostwriter Terry Banker uses the listing method to "expand the possibilities" whenever and however he's stuck.

> Lists help me out of most messes. For example, if I don't know what a character will do next, I create a list (1-10) and I fill in the blanks. The first few are easy answers and generally too simple. By the time I hit 5, 6, and 7, the ideas are flowing. By 9 and 10, I usually have a good or great answer, and one I wouldn't have thought of had my list gone from 1 to 5. Lists get me out of all kinds of problems:

> character choices, scenes to come next, what
> would be the last thing a character would do.
> – Terry Banker, *Underdogs of the Caribbean*

A straightforward way to use the listing technique is to write out all the things that you need to accomplish in the scene where you're stuck. The items on the list can refer to the character's arc, the plot, the setting, theme, laying clues, foreshadowing the ending, or any combo of elements you desire. It might look something like the list below that I made for a scene (in a story I'm not actually writing) in which I don't know how my hero will escape from a dungeon.

What I need to accomplish in this scene is:

1. get him out of the dungeon;

2. have him get himself out rather than being rescued;

3. have him use a skill he's recently learned to get himself out;

4. foreshadow the climax of the story when he rescues the princess;

5. have him face his claustrophobia;

6. have him fail before he succeeds;

7. show him emotionally processing through this failure and learning from it;

8. provide some humorous relief.

After making this list, not only do I have a better handle on what I'm trying to accomplish, I have an inspiration: I stopped listing when I got to "humorous relief" because that sparked an idea for introducing a tame rat into the scene. Something funny could happen with the rat that jogs my hero out of his funk over his previous failures and/or gives him a brilliant insight into a new escape plan.

Now I'm excited, I'm inspired, and I'm writing. I write the part where the hero is claustrophobic. I write the failed escape attempts. I write him into an emotional funk over his failures. I write the appearance of the tame rat who hands the hero an old nail, presumably trying to help him escape. The hero laughs. He's out of his funk and the nail sparks an amazing, brilliant, fantastic, perfect escape plan...

And now I'm stuck again. I still have no idea how he's going to escape, so I'll make another list. This time I'll list all the options I can think of for using the nail to escape.

1. use the nail to pick the lock on the door;

2. tunnel out through the rock wall with the nail, but it takes a hundred years;

3. throw the nail out of the cell, perfectly hitting a fire alarm button; when the fire alarm goes off, the cell door springs open;

4. start a fire with a spark from scraping the nail on a rock; the fire brings guards who open the door; he fights them and escapes;

5. use the nail to kill the rat, then eat the rat gaining strength from the nourishment—no wait, gaining the rat's magical powers, which he uses to escape;

6. the nail reminds him of the time he hit his finger with a hammer and the finger swelled, giving him the idea to blow up the rat like a giant balloon, putting pressure on the cell door until the lock breaks and the door opens;

7. the nail reminds him of the summer he spent learning dungeon construction from his uncle; he remembers some detail about construction that enables him to see a weak point in the dungeon's structure, which he exploits in order to escape.

Note how the list started with the most obvious, progressed to the impossible, then to the ridiculous, then finally to an idea I could use.

When award-winning writer Brandy Vallance makes lists to get unstuck, she too finds value in including the ridiculous and processing past it.

> When I'm stuck on a plot point I make a "Stream of Consciousness List" of everything that could happen next, including the most ridiculous thing possible. I literally write: [hero, heroine] flies to moon, is abducted by aliens …Usually by the time I reach the end of the page I have a useable idea and the story can go on. For me this is about giving myself permission to "let go."
> – Brandy Vallance, *The Covered Deep*

Though Banker suggests a list of ten, and Vallance doesn't specify a target number, the prolific group of writers, Rose-Colored Ink, recommends making a list of twenty when doing this exercise.

Members of Rose-Colored Ink use this list-making method often when brainstorming together, and they always recommend it to writers who are stuck. They specify twenty as the target number because they find that it usually takes them at least ten items to get through all the common and obvious ideas. After ten it gets harder to come up with things, and somewhere in the fifteen to twenty range is where they usually produce the "coolest" options.

Karen Fox is a founding member of Rose-Colored Ink who uses the list method any time she gets stalled or stuck:

> I use it mostly for figuring out things that could happen within the context of the plot. For example, when I was writing *Guardians of the Gate: Through the Mirror*, I had a good framework, but I didn't have enough plot points, and I had a really saggy middle. I made a list to explore what could happen in the story to provide more action and tension. While I was making the list, I kept at the forefront of my mind that I wanted to make things really difficult for my character, so I pushed myself harder to make the bad things worse.

This is the list of twenty that Karen produced. The ideas she ended up using are starred.

1. Ash helps her learn to move things in real world;*
2. Sister gets worse;*
3. They lose battle at gate;

4. Tries to fight demon in real world and fails;*

5. Finds her demon and can't kill it;

6. Her parents are falling apart;

7. She goes on hunting expeditions, some good, some bad;

8. She's wounded in battle;

9. She fights with Quinn;

10. Tessa's story;

11. Quinn's story;*

12. Dickson's story;

13. Amanda sends her to demon central;

14. Fights with Amanda;

15. Gets trapped in real world—fading;

16. Loses sword;

17. Spends time with Ash;*

18. Demon tries to get Ash, her parents and/or Molly;*

19. Meets Gabriel;*

20. Goes hunting by herself.*

> This list gave me enough ideas to pull that story together, plus gave me inspiration for the next book in the series.
> – Karen Fox, "Blood Rising," *Magick Rising*

Next time you find yourself stuck, make a list and check it twice. And don't forget to include the ridiculous.

34. PLAY "WHAT IF?"

Romantic suspense and mystery writer Donnell Ann Bell has been stuck on everything from rough drafts to final polishes. On one notable occasion, her editor made a "small" request that had Donnell stuck in a big way:

> For *The Past Came Hunting*, in the version I turned in to my editor, I had my protagonist take a gun out of storage and place it on the top shelf of her closet to show the reader that she was afraid. My editor asked what the character does with the gun. "Nothing," I replied. "She can't because she's an ex-convict. Even possessing a firearm is a violation of her parole." My editor was entirely unsympathetic. "Do something with that gun," she said. That was a problem for me because I'm such a rule follower. I had no idea what the protagonist should do with the gun, and my editor didn't tell me how to fix it, she just said to fix it.

So what did Donnell do to get unstuck?

> I started playing "what if" scenarios. What if I make her face her attacker and she actually

has to use it? What if she gets caught with the gun, which would be a terrible conflict between my heroine and the hero, who happens to be a police lieutenant who lives next door? Or what if her son gets hold of the gun? *Voilà*. That was all I needed to give my protagonist the motivation to come clean with her neighbor police officer. She loved her son far more than she was afraid of violating parole or going back to prison. I had my answer, and the scene I wrote turned out great—loaded with emotion and conflict. "What if" scenarios are an invaluable way of getting unstuck.

– Donnell Ann Bell, *Betrayed*

So if you're stuck, ask yourself some questions about your story, and observe how your answers affect your story plan. You may uncover a hidden gem that gets you rolling on your story again.

Here are some questions to start you out:

- What if you change the age of your protagonist? Antagonist?

- What if you change the gender?

- What if your character wasn't in the story at all? Whose story would it be? How would it be different?

- What if the story were told from a different point-of-view? Whose? How would that change the story? Would it change the theme? Would it change the ending?

- What if you changed the setting to a different time period or place?

- What would happen if you removed a pivotal event or a chapter? How would that change things? (If your answer is "not at all," leave it out!)

- What if your character dies at the end? Or if you're planning for the character to die, what if s/he lives? Does that change how you look at the whole story?

- What if at present your point-of-view character is ancient and on his/her deathbed, and the story is him/her looking back? How would this change things?

- What if your character is dead and looking back at his/her life from the afterlife?

The "what if" game can be even better when played with a partner. That person doesn't have to be a writer, but if s/he is, you can take turns playing "what if" with each other's stories. If that writer is someone you are co-writing a story with, even better:

> One of the best things about writing with a partner is that you have someone else, who completely understands your story, to help you get unstuck. We find using "what if?" works even better with two people, and we also find that you need to keep pushing until you have a lot of "what ifs." The higher the quantity, the more likely it is we'll come up with something we can use.
> —Mary Lee Woods and Anita Carter
> writing as Sparkle Abbey

Try having someone else ask you "what if" questions about your story. Pay attention to the contortions your brain does when trying to answer them. What insights do you gain? If you have a visceral, negative reaction to a concept, pay close attention: you've hit a nerve that you might benefit from exploring.

Remember that this exercise is intended to broaden your perspective on your story and see what develops from re-imagining choices you've made. The "what if" questions are not suggestions for how you *should* change your story; they're merely food for thought.

35. ON THIS DAY IN HISTORY

One of my more quirky techniques for getting unstuck is to select a famous event from history to ponder in the context of your story. Whether you choose an event at random, or you carefully select one that speaks to you, ask yourself how you could incorporate a similar scenario into your story. Chances are the details won't mesh, but try looking at the event symbolically. Viewed this way, can you imagine how a situation like that could become a scene for your protagonist? Or your antagonist? Try writing a scene in the historical period, then write one in your story's setting.

My writing buddy, Bonnie Hagan, was stuck on a scene and, good friend that she is, agreed to try this offbeat exercise. In the interest of full disclosure, I'll share that Bonnie had no great hopes for any "magic" to come from this. She intended to treat it as a sort of perfunctory exercise to help me come up with an anecdote for this book. *But when she did the exercise...*I'll let Bonnie tell you what happened in her own words because she does a far better job than I could. Plus this way it sounds a lot less like tooting my own horn.

So, I'd been having trouble with a scene for a while. It's a hard scene in several ways. First, the scene occurs halfway through the novel, but it's the first time a new POV [point-of-view] is introduced. Second, the new POV character, Margaret, is from a completely different time (Philadelphia, 1849) than my main protagonist (Colorado Springs, present day). Third, Margaret is traveling to a new world via magic—something the reader has already seen my main protagonist do; and meeting the supposed Big Bad Guy—also something my protagonist has already done. So I faced lots of challenges trying to make this scene resonate and remain interesting to the reader.

My process for creating this scene started with an exorbitant amount of research on Philadelphia in the 1840s. Then I'd done character research and tried to understand Margaret both as a person and in terms of character and theme. Armed with all of this— not to mention a ton of nineteenth century lingo—I carefully layered words across the page. It fell flat. I couldn't figure out what I was missing, but the scene just wasn't working. It was almost, but not quite, as inspiring as the instructions on a bottle of shampoo.

Enter the "Unstuck" exercise to select a famous historical event. Instantly a plethora of events popped into my head, but they were all wars or assassinations, neither of which spoke to me. So, I decided to let Google play a part in this, and I entered "famous historical events America" into the search engine. I clicked on the first result—a top ten list. Sure enough, it brought up wars and assassinations, and as I scrolled, I became more disappointed. Until I reached the number one event on the list: the moon landing.

All I needed were those three words: The Moon Landing. In my story, Margaret is traveling to a new world via magic. Well, great day in the morning, if that's not exactly what the astronauts were doing in 1969. Following the dictates of the exercise, I wrote my Margaret into the Moon Landing. She took the place of Buzz Aldrin alongside Neil Armstrong on that fateful journey. What I learned as I wrote this was the sense of magic and wonder that would come with visiting a new place by strange means.

I realized what I'd been missing in my own story. I rewrote my scene, and instantly both the micro-tension and the readability increased just from injecting this sense of adventure. Fortunately, I could still use my lovely vocabulary and character research, but the important elements were wonder and fear. As a writer, I needed to capture for the reader the spirit of this moment and not bury it in an avalanche of "vital plot elements." This exercise took a scene that languished under the weight of its own importance and made it just a little afraid and more than a little amazed.

– Bonnie Hagan, *Raveling*

If this doesn't inspire you to try this exercise, I'm not sure what would. Thanks, Bonnie!

36. Ask a Character

Ask a character? Are you kidding? They're not real!

It may sound silly, but talking to your characters and listening to their replies can actually work to get you unstuck, even if you're not the flavor of writer who believes their characters speak to them.

Go ahead and try it. Think about where you're stuck, and ask the point-of-view character in that scene about it. You can ask your character questions mentally, verbally or on the page.

A good question to begin with is: "What do you want in this scene?"

Whatever answer pops into your head, grab onto it, even if it surprises you, even if you don't fully understand it. Follow up with more questions, especially if you're surprised by what s/he wants.

For example, you can ask "I thought you wanted X. Do you want this new thing more than you want X? Was I wrong about you wanting X?"

You can even ask point-blank about the thing you're stuck on: "Why won't you do X like I want you to?"

Sometimes your character "knows" that a certain plotline is not appropriate, or a certain action is out of character, but for whatever reason you-as-the-writer don't see it.

When my critique partner, Todd Fahnestock, got stuck on a scene, he didn't think to ask his character why he was stuck, but he did think to call me. Our conversation went something like this:

"Chris, I'm stuck. I've been writing a scene for*effing*ever and I'm about ready to print it out and light it on fire."

"What's going on?"

"This *effing* character won't do what I say."

"Have you asked him why?" I asked.

"Excuse me?

"Humor me and ask him."

"Damn you."

"What?"

"He answered me."

"That didn't take long. What did he say?"

"He said he never runs from a fight. He said the fact that *I* need him to leave the battle is nowhere near enough reason for him to leave."

"I guess he told you," I said. "So if you really need him to leave the fight, give him a stronger motivation."

"Damn you."

"What now?"

"You're right."

I like being right, but more than that, I like helping writers get unstuck, and I've found that a big reason writers get stuck is that they're trying to make a character do something that *the writer* needs, rather than something that the character wants or needs. Asking your character is a great way to illuminate this difference, and to remedy it.

Conversing with your character can absolutely take the form of asking him questions directly and then answering yourself as the character, but talking to your characters doesn't have to be that specific:

> Sometimes when I'm blocked on what comes next in a piece of fiction I go to a park or a mall, some busy place with lots of people, conversation, things to see. I program myself that I will see or overhear something which will tell me the next event or bit of conversation in my story—I imagine it's a way my characters use to tell me things.
> – Steve Rasnic Tem, *Blood Kin*

When you're stuck, try asking your character about it, and your questions might just be answered.

37. ASK A WRITER

There's more than one way to ask a writer. This exercise will highlight two ways that are so different from each other, they might as well be opposites:

1. The "want ad," or the *specific* ask
2. Blue-skying, or the *general* ask

Consult The "Want Ads"

Sometimes when we're stuck, we think we know exactly what we're stuck on and exactly what we need in order to get unstuck. And sometimes we're right.

If you are stuck in such a way that you need something very specific to get you unstuck—like a plot point, a weapon, a name—create a "want ad" with a "job description" for the missing element. Include as much information as necessary for other writers to understand what you're looking for.

Let's pretend I'm looking for a name for an antagonist. I might write a "want ad" like this:

```
Wanted: first name for villain in epic fantasy
novel. Name should be one syllable and cannot
begin with the letters J, L, P, or V (due to the
```

names of other main characters). The ethnic "feel" of the name could lean toward Germanic or Scandinavian, but all ethnic leanings will be given equal consideration. Name should connote cleverness, ruthlessness, deceit, and/or darkness. Applicants must go well with the surname "Geier" (which means "vulture"). Happy, sunny names need not apply.

Sometimes thinking about the problem in this specific manner is all it takes to be able to produce the answer yourself. But if it doesn't, send the job description out to other writers and ask them to "apply." The right candidate might show up in the mail.

Mardra Sikora tried this exercise with her critique group. After the members wrote their ads, they read them aloud. Mardra said that this facilitated a discussion about the varied blocks that members were facing, and how to overcome them. It was particularly helpful for those who had a hard time identifying how they were stuck because the exercise forced them to put it into words while the rest of the group was there to help them.

Mardra wasn't stuck at the time, so she used the exercise to focus her thoughts on her next big writing task:

Wanted: Second book in series. Must have tension and forward momentum sufficient to appease large audiences of typical fantasy readers. Story must also confirm within each page the theme of the value of life. There must be villains that are hate-worthy yet human. There must be heroes that have relatable flaws yet enviable courage. Heroes must also be examples of our better selves while still struggling with fears and misunderstandings that are part of the human condition. It is

```
preferred that the book chapters arrive in the
order of the story time-line, but not required.
Books should apply via conscious hours and provide
relief and comfort to both readers and the writer.
```

Even through Mardra wasn't stuck when she did the exercise, she shares that she benefited in two ways:

> A) It made me feel good. I got that endorphin rush that comes from simply acknowledging my goals. B) It provided me with a big picture template of what I want to accomplish in book two.

Sometimes it's great to look at specifics, asking yourself or other writers specific questions like with a "want ad." But sometimes this specific thinking can serve to stifle brainstorming, leaving you feeling boxed in, painted into a corner, or led down a blind alley. The pressure to come up with a specific solution can make you feel even more stuck. And what if you're wrong about what you need? You could ask all year for that specific thing, and still be stuck.

In these cases, I recommend trying the opposite and asking for help in a totally non-specific way: blue-skying.

Blue-Sky It

The terms "blue-skying" and "blue-sky thinking" are often used in business settings to refer to the process of stepping back from an issue and brainstorming the big picture with an open mind.

To blue-sky what you're stuck on, find another writer to brainstorm with. Explain where you are in the project, what you're trying to accomplish, and what you're stuck on. Talk it over from all angles, no holds barred. The key is to consider everything, and not be focused on any one element, issue, requirement, or concept.

The beauty of blue-skying with another writer is that we speak the same language. Writers know how to ask the right questions. We understand the expectations of the craft, and are familiar with the goals and challenges common in fiction writing. We get it.

> When I'm floundering about what I'm going to write next, I often call a critique partner and brainstorm plot ideas.
> – Diana Cosby, international bestselling author of Scottish medieval romantic suspense

One of my favorite things to do with my critique partners is blue-sky sticking points in our stories. Sometimes we do it as part of a critique group meeting, while other times we'll talk one-on-one. Recently my partner, Aaron Brown, was struggling through the denouement of his novel, *Bigger*. He couldn't figure out how to get his protagonist, Caleb, through a series of difficult challenges at the end of the book. He felt like he was slogging through the mud, that the remaining scenes were a drag and a downer, when all Aaron wanted to do was tie up the loose ends quickly.

After a whole lot of blue-skying the situation, we discovered the problem: Aaron was writing the "old" Caleb, the person Caleb used to be before he experienced the life-changing climax of the book. But the scenes in question take place after the climax, when Caleb is a changed man.

The key question turned out to be: "How would the *new* Caleb regard his duties at the end?"

Aaron's answer: "Like a gift. He'd view them as a gift, not a burden, not an obligation."

And just like that, Aaron was off and running, writing the scenes with an entirely different emotional perspective.

38. ASK AN EXPERT

Somewhere someone is an expert in something related to your story, and that special someone may hold the key to getting you unstuck.

You can find an expert who can speak to pretty much any area where you're stuck. Sometimes it's as simple as using your Internet search engine to find a subject matter expert, and then reaching out with your questions.

For example, if you're stuck writing a scene about the Battle of Gettysburg because you don't know anything about the Colt M1849 revolver your character would have used, there are experts on that gun who would absolutely love to chat with you by phone or email. After all, how often does this expert get to share—with an eager listener—details about how much "kick" that gun has, what malfunctions it commonly had in the field, and how much it was likely to cost in 1863? And no matter where this expert is in the world, s/he's as close as a Web search.

A great way to find expert advice is by word of mouth—asking members of your family, critique groups, clubs, and friends to refer you to someone with expertise in your area of interest. Recently when author M.J. Brett was drafting her tenth novel, she got stuck writing a character with Post Traumatic Stress Disorder. M.J. had no idea how a soldier with PTSD would think, feel, or act in the scenario of a particular scene she was writing, and her Web searches hadn't yielded anything useful. What she needed was a personal contact, someone she could talk to one-on-one. M.J. put the word out that she was looking for an expert on PTSD. That same day a writer-friend responded, putting M.J. in touch with a nurse who runs a nonprofit helping soldiers with PTSD. Problem solved. Writer unstuck.

Other times you may need to go a bit further afield to find an "expert." For example, middle grade author M.J. Stewart is a self-described "old lady" whose characters are teenaged snowboarders. While M.J. is a seasoned skier, she's out of touch with the snowboarder culture. She was stuck on her novel, *Two Degrees from Zero*, because she couldn't capture the voice of the characters and the feel of the teen snowboarding scene. So she asked an expert. She strapped on her skis and caught a chairlift up the mountain, making sure she was seated with a teen boarder. She played it cool as a curious grandmother-type, not an undercover writer, and she got a few shreddin' phrases to include in her book. She skied down the run and rode back up the lift with another boarder. Then another. She grew bolder and started asking questions, requesting explanations of phrases, and posing specific story scenarios to her captive experts. It paid off: she got the hang of the lingo, the culture, and the voice. What's more, she knew that if she got stuck again, the answer was only as far as the nearest chairlift or board shop.

Author Ronald Cree found an expert very close to home: his son. Ron's first novel had a Latino cast of characters and a fair amount of Spanish dialogue, which meant that Ron was frequently stuck because he's not Latino and doesn't speak Spanish. When that happened, Ron's adopted son Gabriel, who is Mexican, would coach him through the rough patches.

> Getting the characters to feel authentic and speak realistically was a huge challenge for me, and the writing would often come to a complete standstill as I struggled to get through a scene. When I enlisted Gabriel's help, he'd stay quiet while I explained the trouble spot, deeply contemplating whatever I was telling him. Then he'd gently start picking things apart, pointing out where I got things wrong. This was usually related to the Latino lifestyle, the Spanish language, or the way Mexican-Americans would really behave in a particular situation. He was very good at it, taking an almost professorial approach in the way he explained things.

> Once instance I remember clearly was a scene where my teen character, Gus, was having an intense conversation with his adopted father in the father's room. It was late when the discussion ended, so Gus threw some blankets down to sleep on the floor next to his father's

bed. When Gabriel heard that, he couldn't believe it. "Why doesn't he sleep in the bed with his dad?" he asked, truly confused. I reminded him it was a teen book and that would likely be frowned upon. "Then you're not writing real characters," he scolded. "That's not the way Mexicans do it. We can't sleep at all if we're not piled on top of one another." This line later made it into the book, as did many of Gabriel's funny and heartbreaking anecdotes about his life on the border, crossing the desert with his brothers, *phantasmas*, coyotes (the human kind), and *chicas*. Talking to Gabriel truly was the best way to get unstuck.

– Ronald Cree, *Desert Blood 10pm/9c*

If you were to have access to an expert in an area pertaining to your book, what would you ask? Make a list of questions. Pose some "what if" scenarios. Don't forget the mundane—those things you assume or have taken for granted but may have gotten wrong. Then actually try to find an expert and contact them. Try for a face-to-face meeting or a phone call. If that's not possible, write a letter via email or snail mail.

If you can't locate an expert who will help you, ask *yourself* the questions you've prepared for the expert, then research the answers. That's what award-winning novelist Debbie Allen did when she got stuck writing the setting for a novel set in Croatia. She figured out what "expert" information she needed, then she went to work answering her own questions via the Internet and books.

I'm terrible at imagining a storyworld, and my plot can drag (along with my description) as a result. For one book, I needed a castle. I tried to create one out of my imagination, but that went nowhere. To get unstuck I began researching castles. After some digging, I found one in particular that was perfect for my needs. It had been turned into a museum, so all the floor plans were available, as well as tons of pictures of the interior and exterior. I chose that castle for my setting, and was able to research the answers to all my questions via the images and information I found on the Internet and in books. As a bonus, some of the rooms I saw in photographs inspired scenes in the book I hadn't envisioned before, like the "Hall of Portraits" where the forbidding red walls are lined with the images of sour-faced royals.

— Debbie Allen, *SpindleWish*

If, despite all your research, you can't find an answer, make it up based on the other information you've learned. Construct an outline or cheat sheet with real facts that bolster your fictional answer, then think about how you'd defend your answer if you were challenged on its veracity.

However you arrive at the expert answers—through an actual expert, doing research, or via your own imagination—you'll know a lot more about the area you're stuck on than when you started. Hopefully a detail or tidbit of information you discovered along the way will help you move past your block with ease.

39. ASK THE OPPOSITION

When you're stuck, do a one-eighty and check out what's in the opposite direction. Turn the story problem upside down. Reverse it, as Terry Banker does:

> Often after I've written myself into a corner, I reverse expectations to become unstuck. For example, what is the last thing a reader would expect (within the rules of my story)? What is the last thing my protagonist would ever do? If he would never think about betraying his father, I create a situation where he must betray his father. By reversing an idea and exploring the outcomes of opposite motivations, not only do I get unstuck but the new multidimensional characteristics that emerge lead me to more original and complex characters.
>
> – Terry Banker, author, ghostwriter,
> and story consultant

Editor Tiffany Yates Martin frequently sees writers get stuck when they're trying to force a story to go where it doesn't "want" to go. That's when she recommends they try the opposite.

I am a believer that you can't force a vision on a story. If you've created real, vivid characters and a juicy situation, eventually it takes on a life of its own. When this happens, if you try to impose your will over the will of the characters, they freeze up. They boycott you. When your characters refuse to perform because you have written the story into a corner it doesn't want to be in, I recommend writing a scene—even just a throwaway scene—where the exact opposite thing happens.

Do you want your protagonist to leave her husband and run away with her lover? Then make her find out she's pregnant and can't leave. Or give her husband a terminal illness so she can't abandon him. Or make her lover discover his ex is pregnant and he won't leave her. Take the thing that ruins the story you are trying to tell—directly flies in the face of your intentions—and write the scene that way.

The scene you write may not be where the story ultimately goes. It probably won't be if you use extreme, bodice-ripping, melodramatic examples like I did. But that's the idea! Take the craziest, most completely opposite thing you can think of and write it, just as an exercise. More often than not, even though you won't use that actual idea, it will jostle something loose, and you'll see an avenue out of your blind alley.

–Tiffany Yates Martin, FoxPrint Editorial

The next time your characters boycott you, make it "opposite day." Put your shirt on backwards, sit on the wrong side of your desk, and turn your character on his head by writing a scene where you take what you think needs to happen and write the opposite. After all, if the pennies won't come out the bottom of your precious porcelain childhood keepsake piggy bank, what do you do? You turn it upside down and give it a good shake. Better yet, take a hammer to it because that's that last thing anyone would expect.

PART FIVE:
MIND OPENERS—
GETTING IN THE ZONE

The Zone: that lovely state where creativity flows freely through you, and thoughts and ideas come so rapidly you can't record them fast enough. I know you know what I'm talking about. You've been there at least once. But can you go there at will? Some writers can. Others of us use tricks and exercises to get there. That's okay. There's no shame in that.

When we reach The Zone naturally, it may be during a specific time of day when we feel extra creative, or it could be the result of going to a place that feels magical and inspiring. Have you noticed certain times or places that induce this creative state in you? Pay attention to the circumstances next time you find yourself in The Zone because repeating those circumstances can help induce that state of mind next time you need it.

Still not sure how to get in The Zone? Don't worry. The exercises in this section are designed to blast through (or sneak past) the mental and emotional barriers between you and The Zone.

To get in The Zone, typically you must find a way to quiet the "other things" in your mind. So fair warning: if you have not yet mastered shutting up your inner critic, you may find him/her interfering with this process.

Also note that "avoiders" of writing will probably find these exercises to be merely additional ways to avoid writing. To counter this, be intentional when you do the exercises. In other words, when you're approaching or in The Zone, *think about your story.* Let your mind wander, but keep it within the parameters of your story world.

Learning how to get in The Zone—a place of pure creativity where ideas flow plentifully, thoughts come easily, and there are no wrong answers—is one of the best things you can do to overcome writer's block because:

> In the creative process, sometimes pure creativity is the only way.
> — Stephen W. Saffel DEO,
> Senior Acquisitions Editor, Titan Books

40. WATER TREATMENT

There's one place I get more brainstorms than anywhere else: the shower. If I'm stuck and I *can* take a shower, I do. Of course if I'm writing at a café or a friend's house, this isn't always practical. But when nothing else is working to get me unstuck, showering almost always does the trick.

Kendra Merritt, 2014 winner of the Pikes Peak Writers "Zebulon" contest in the Science Fiction and Fantasy category, shares a recent breakthrough she experienced in the shower:

> I had trouble with a caricature of Sigmund Freud in my novel, *A Shroud for My Bride*. He was super fun to write, but in the end I realized he represented the opposite view of what I wanted to present in the book. A week of brainstorming didn't fix the problem, leaving me with dead-end scenes and boring dialogue. A couple friends had good suggestions but it wasn't until I was washing my hair one morning that the solution jostled itself loose. With soap in my eyes, I figured out how to keep Freud and parallel him with another character, one

who actually supported the things I wanted to
say with my novel.

I can't tell you with any real authority the technical or
psychological reasons why showering works to get
unstuck, but I suspect it's due to a combination of
isolation, relaxation, and "rote" activity that doesn't
require much conscious thought.

Writer Jared Hagan says he doesn't get "stuck," but once
in a while he does get "paused," and when he does:

> I find that a hot shower frees my mind and
> solves my problems. I'm completely away from
> distractions. I'm comfortable. I don't feel guilty
> for being there (like I should be doing so many
> other things). So I can think without guilt or
> distraction. The steam clears my head and my
> story's knots wash away. Then I dry off and get
> back to writing, feeling refreshed. The main
> reason I think this works for me, besides the
> lack of distractions, is that I am able to act out
> scenes without feeling self-conscious. I can
> become any character, or multiple characters,
> and talk out a conversation, feeling what is
> motivating each one and what they would
> naturally say as a result.

Though I don't make a habit of showering with other
writers, I have asked a lot of writers where they get their
brainstorms, and "the shower" is by far the most
common answer. I've also asked physicists, teachers,
artists, and managerial sorts where they experience the
most/best brainstorms, and they concur: the shower.

So next time you're stuck or looking for your next great brainstorm, give yourself the water treatment—it often creates *showers* of ideas.

41. HOUSEHOLD HELP

> Do something that isn't writing, but let the
> writing roll around in your head.
> —Stephen W. Saffel DEO,
> Senior Acquisitions Editor, Titan Books

Tackling household chores—like dishes, laundry, or washing the baseboards—can be a great way to get unstuck when you let your story "roll around in your head" as Saffel recommends. Chores that require more conscious thought—like cooking or filing—aren't always as conducive to story-pondering as monotonous, repetitive chores like scrubbing, vacuuming, or even painting.

While doing your chore of choice, let your story be the only thing between you and boredom, and see what bubbles up from your subconscious. Beware of looking too hard at your story "problem" or the area where you're stuck, as this can sometimes scare inspiration away. I prefer to hold my story loosely in my mind and let my imagination play.

Multi-published author and journalist Maria Faulconer got stuck writing the climax of a young adult suspense novel about a girl who is kidnapped by a violent predator. She felt that, given the nature of the situation, the only realistic conclusion was to have the police swoop in and save the girl. But every attempt to write that scene fell flat.

> I knew I had to step away from the computer, so I foraged in the refrigerator—my first go-to strategy when I'm stuck—but that didn't help. I watched a mindless TV show, but that didn't help either. Then I spied the dreaded laundry basket with several of my husband's wrinkled shirts piled on top. I hate to iron. But I couldn't think of anything else to do. In desperation, I pulled out the ironing board and plugged in the iron. After spritzing the shirt with water, I set the iron on top of the shirt. As I moved the iron back and forth, back and forth along the shirt, I focused on my story, and a strange thing happened. I had a mind shift.
>
> By the time I got to the collar, I realized that my main character had to take control of her own destiny and do everything she could to save herself. At the end of the day, she may not be totally successful, but she had to make the effort. And her boyfriend, who was crazy with worry about her, needed to be hot on her trail. After that breakthrough, the climax virtually wrote itself. The only drawback was I didn't do a great job ironing that shirt. I'll still do anything to get out of ironing under most circumstances, but when I'm stuck, my first go-to strategy is now to plug in that iron.
>
> — Maria Faulconer, *A Mom for Umande*

I personally find that doing mindless chores almost always works to break through a block. On the rare occasion when it doesn't, it's not a total loss: at least I got some chores done.

42. THE EXERCISE EXERCISE

Exercise. Some of us hate it, some of us love it. Either way, it can work miracles when it comes to getting unstuck and staying that way.

I find that the best kind of exercise for opening the mind to write is activity that is solitary and monotonous. Things like running on a treadmill or around a track, hiking (in a familiar place), climbing stadium stairs, using a stair-stepper or elliptical machine, cross country skiing or biking (or the gym equivalent), and swimming.

Exercises where you have to count reps, think about where you are going, or interact with others might interfere with getting in, and staying in, the creative zone. But everyone is different, so whatever exercise you prefer to get your blood flowing, why not see if it gets your creative juices flowing, too?

> I start every morning with an early walk. I use part of that time to remember where I left off in yesterday's writing session and to envision what I want to accomplish that day.
>
> – Anne Hillerman,
> *Spider Woman's Daughter*

Going for a walk is by far the most popular way of getting in The Zone among writers I know.

Author Aaron Ritchey, who himself is a big fan of going for walks to ponder his stories, points out that writers who walk as part of the creative process are in good company with Kirkegaard, Nietzsche, Dickens, and H.P. Lovecraft. Ritchey says that for him, walking is the best way to get out of his own head and into his story, and a great way to get unstuck.

> When I'm stuck, when the next scene doesn't come, or when I need to fix something I know is broken, I walk out the problem. For example, when I wrote *The Never Prayer*, I came up short in word count. More important than that, I knew the story needed another layer of conflict. I had a secondary villain that did a lot of posturing and "I'm gonna get all evil someday" but didn't actually do anything. I knew this villain could provide the extra conflict and words I needed, but I didn't know how to tie it all together. So I went for a walk.

> This is what happens: I walk. I get bored. I start telling myself stories. The story I told myself that day was the story of the secondary villain. It involved insanity and bombs and lockers and cell phones. I got the word count up, I got another layer of conflict, and the ending turned out better than I'd originally planned. It was a much better book.

> I also walked out the plot in *Long Live the Suicide King*. When I started walking, all I had

was a great start: my hero encounters a barking little dog. But then what? I walked, got bored, and told myself the story. It took eight miles, but I plotted the entire book.
– Aaron Michael Ritchey,
Long Live the Suicide King

Rachael Dahl also walks to get unstuck, but she adds an additional component: she walks with weights in her hands, pumping them while she thinks. She recalls a time when she was stuck on a scene where she wanted to show a more human side to her antagonist, but she couldn't come up with a noble deed that would fit with his personality and his evil ways. She was on a deadline, and starting to panic.

It was worse than a blank slate! So I grabbed my three-pound weights and walked around my living room, pumping the dumbbells up, down, side-to-side, letting my mind wander. Within a few minutes, I had it. He would plant trees for the community because he'd used lumber when killing one of his victims. This totally fit because of how important cosmic balance is to him. I ditched my weights and within forty minutes pounded out the entire scene.
– Rachael Dahl, *Shattered Lives*

If you were to ask Aaron Michael Ritchey what to do when you're stuck, he'd tell you: "Walk and walk and walk. The mind will clear, perhaps you'll get a little bored. And then the storytelling begins."

But if it turns out that walking—or whatever exercise you choose—doesn't serve to get your story ideas flowing, at least your blood will be flowing a little faster when you sit back down to write. Sometimes that's all it takes to get in that creative zone where the words flow faster than you can type them.

43. ROAD TRIP!

I love a good road trip. I can see it in my mind's eye: the open highway stretched out in front of me all the way to the horizon. I'm sure you can picture this if you've ever driven across Kansas, Nevada, or Texas, which I have. But even in more populated areas, like Denver, San Francisco, or Atlanta, I can always find a back road to take a leisurely drive.

Why am I telling you this? Because taking a drive is one of the best ways I've found to break through a block. If you don't drive, that's okay. Being a passenger in a car, bus, plane, or train can work, too.

The idea behind this is to clear your mind of distractions and "shoulds" by giving yourself the job of driving (or riding) along a route that doesn't take much conscious thought to navigate. By doing this, you're using just a portion of your conscious mind, leaving the rest available. Typically we occupy that available portion of our minds with conversation or music. If you shut down those sources of entertainment, you might fill the void with thoughts of what to make for dinner, what movie to see, how to fix a problem at work, or the making of any number of mental lists of things you need to do. If you can keep these types of thoughts at bay and let your story fill that void instead, you might find yourself with all sorts of ideas. After all, it's that or be bored.

One important consideration: don't attempt to get lost in your story if you're driving in a place that's mentally challenging to negotiate. For example, I wouldn't recommend this exercise if you're driving through Boston or L.A.

That said, driving someplace that requires a great deal of focus works wonders to get J.T. Evans unstuck. He says that's because if he's blocked, it's usually due to his tendency to "overthink" things, and turning that hyper-focus to something else is the only thing that breaks the analysis paralysis.

> The laser-sharp focus on hard driving forces everything else from my brain. After driving this way for 20-30 minutes, it's like a good plumber has roto-rooted out my synapses. That's when I slow down, turn on the cruise control, and relax. Then I take a leisurely drive along the back roads home, allowing thoughts of my story to slowly creep back in. By the time I get home, I have fresh ideas on how to approach the part where I was stuck.
>
> – J.T. Evans,
> "One-Thousand, Eighty Degrees,"
> *Phobias: A Collection of True Stories*

Author Ron Cree has a slightly different take on driving to get unstuck: he road trips with a companion. It started when he was blocked on his first book and he would talk through his story problems in the car with his son. Many years later, with his son now living several states away, Ron continues the tradition, taking drives with friends to brainstorm his stories. Most recently, his novel *Gaap* was born of a conversation with another writer while driving through Rocky Mountain National Park.

> Maybe it's the whole "captive audience" thing while in a car...or maybe it's just the open road, the wind, the passing scenery ...Whatever it is, it works for getting unstuck.
> – Ronald Cree, *Desert Blood 10pm/9c*

44. WRITE SOMETHING, ANYTHING

Most people who come down with a case of the dreaded writer's block are not blocked from writing *everything*. Usually we're stuck on a particular scene, decision, or element. Even when we're stuck in a big way on a whole story, usually we're not so stuck we can't write something on another project. Sometimes by turning our attention to writing something *else*, we can open up our mental pathways and return to the "stuck" place with more success.

So turn to a different project. Try writing a poem. Do an improv writing exercise, some journaling, or a blog post. Write a letter. Heck, even write a descriptive paragraph of what you see in front of you. The idea here is to write something. *Anything*.

Jeff Schmoyer rarely gets writer's block. He attributes this to the fact that when he feels stuck he simply moves on to another task—something he "knows how to write." He says that when he returns to the original problem, his subconscious has usually figured out a way to solve it.

Recently I worked with new writer "Zoe" who was having difficulty writing any fiction at all. She was unsure about her overall story arc, and kept getting stuck whenever she had to make a plot decision. I recommended she borrow a well-loved, time-tested plot pattern from a fairytale, and write that story using her own characters. The idea was for Zoe to experience writing fiction without getting hung up on plot choices. It was hard to convince her to write something intentionally derivative, and I don't blame her—she has tons of her own incredible, innovative ideas. But since she was stuck and couldn't get her own ideas on the page, she eventually accepted this exercise as a stepping stone to getting unstuck. After spending just a few hours writing her own version of Little Red Riding Hood (which was offbeat and hilarious), she found her sea-legs and was able to successfully transition to writing her own stories.

Julia Allen also benefitted from writing derivative fiction in a way that came as a huge surprise to her. At the time, she was already an experienced mystery writer with three manuscripts partially completed. The problem was, she didn't know how to finish these stories. At the suggestion of a friend, she set aside one month to try to accomplish what she never had: completing a novel. To put the pressure on herself, she decided to do this as part of "National Novel Writing Month" (NaNoWriMo), and attempt to write a brand new novel from scratch in thirty days.

To avoid getting stuck in her old rut of not knowing how to finish the story, Julia chose to write a spoof of a popular story she was well-familiar with: *Twilight* by Stephenie Meyer. The fact that this story was not in the mystery genre made it more appealing as an exercise—Julia felt liberated from the complex snarl of mystery elements that had contributed to her previous writing paralysis.

Now Julia knew exactly what to do, and she did it: she completed that novel in thirty days. Finally writing "the end" was gratifying in ways she hadn't imagined, but what shook her very foundation as a writer was discovering she'd fallen head over heels for her vampire hero and the paranormal romance genre. She realized that she didn't want to write mystery. Instead she wanted to write a paranormal romance starring her new hero. But could she ever complete a story of her own? *Yes.* She could and she did, due in large part to having first written something derivative. Who'd have thought such a "trick" would work?

Unfortunately, writer's block is a fickle demon. A trick that works for one person won't necessarily work for another. A technique that gets you unstuck today might not work on the same story tomorrow or work at all for a different story. Sometimes, despite all the tricks and techniques, a writer finds it impossible to write any new words at all—not derivative fiction, not a letter to Grandma, not even a personal ad.

If this happens to you, try not to panic. As a last-ditch effort, we can sometimes trick our mental writing muscles into cooperating by engaging our *physical* writing muscles. Try transcribing a page from a published book (not your own). The act of penning or typing someone else's words may trigger a response that opens you to writing your own words again.

45. *Liberation by Library*

Read. This may seem like the most common-sense advice, but it's often overlooked.

But of course writers read...right?

Well, not always. We sometimes get so wrapped up in our own stories, we forget the joy and inspiration that can come from immersing ourselves in others' words. I think that reading is a particularly sensible and useful thing to do when we're stuck, plus wearing a "reader's hat" for a change can be a lot of fun.

There are four ways to do this exercise, depending on your whims and needs:

- Read something extraordinarily good;
- Read something extraordinarily bad;
- Read targeted subject matter;
- Read anything.

Multi-published novelist Deb Stover has great success getting unstuck using the "read anything" method because for her, it's the *stories* that matter:

> One of the things that has helped me get unstuck is to set aside my own work and read books I have been depriving myself of due to time constraints. I also will indulge in movie binges, and spend more time with stories, period. My daughter, Bonnie, and I spend a lot of time at the Public Library. The exposure to more books, which have always been such a huge part of my life, reminds me why I always wanted to write fiction. I still do. Sometimes I need reminding.
>
> – Deb Stover, award-winning author
> of more than twenty novels

If you find that, like Deb, "story" lights your creative fire, reading *anything* can help you get unstuck.

Stacy S. Jensen had been stuck trying to get the "right narrative" for a memoir, so she chose to read a book that tackled similar subject matter to hers, as well as having a narrative tone she thought might be appropriate for her story: *The Fault in Our Stars* by John Green. By reading this book Stacy was able to study how the author dealt with tough medical topics, as well as how he achieved a balance between misery and humor. The humor component was particularly important to Stacy because, as she often has to remind herself while writing this memoir, life isn't all misery, and a book about someone who dies doesn't have to be a "misery memoir"—it's about their life before they die as well.

After reading this targeted book, Stacy had the courage and inspiration to plunge back into writing her own book again. Seeing how another writer deftly handled a story with that particular subject matter and tone was exactly what she needed to get unstuck.

Another tactic is to read a book that's extraordinarily good. If reading your own writing often enrages your inner critic, be particularly careful to select a book that does not awaken that critic. By reading something extraordinarily good, you are more likely to achieve total immersion in the story: suspension of disbelief *and* suspension of the inner critic. When you get lost in the fictional world, swept up by the momentum of the narrative and the unraveling of the plot, you can become so engrossed that you're no longer conscious of the fact you're reading. The words and the pages disappear, and what remains is pure story.

I find that being immersed in a novel to this degree while reading is very similar to the feeling of being in The Zone while writing. I believe if you can experience this as a reader, you may be able to recapture the feeling when writing. Plus there's something about reading an extraordinarily good book that can inspire the desire to create one.

Remember that the key to this variant of the exercise is to avoid reading anything that triggers your inner editor. If you are questioning word choice, evaluating sentence structure, or in any way critiquing the work, you have chosen the wrong book.

The final variant of this exercise is to purposefully engage your inner critic by reading something extraordinarily bad. I've talked to several writers—who prefer to remain nameless—who find that reading badly written books can pump up their confidence in their own writing. When they're discouraged about ever achieving writing success, they read a terrible book and then say to themselves: "*I* can do much better than this." This inspires them to return to their own writing with renewed vigor and confidence.

Another way that reading an extraordinarily bad book can help is when you're stuck revising your own work and can't make yourself cut anything. Not only will reading a badly written book wake up your inner editor, but recognizing that someone else's story could have benefited from aggressive editing can prompt you to push harder on your own revisions.

Whatever tack you take on this exercise, the bottom line is (say it with me now) *read*.

46. MOVING PICTURES

For this exercise, watch a movie to get unstuck. This one sounds like a crock, right? You watch movies all the time and it's never helped you get unstuck. What gives?

The difference here is in your *intent*, and in which movie you choose.

To get unstuck, select a movie that is particularly inspiring to you as a writer, like a comedy with such great dialogue that you're amazed and impressed by the writer even after watching it ten times. Or choose the seminal movies in your genre. Or a movie that takes place in a setting similar to yours.

While watching your chosen film, keep in mind *why* you are watching. When you feel the spark of inspiration, hit "pause" and jot down your thoughts or sit back and let your mind play with your story ideas. Whatever you do, don't allow yourself to get swept up in the movie's story.

The minute you forget why you are doing this exercise is the minute it stops being an exercise.

Paranormal writer Kristi Lloyd shares that her first encounter with writer's block was after the character "Chaz" materialized in her manuscript. Kristi had no intention of having a romantic turn to the story, but when she closed her eyes to visualize what happened next to her protagonist, Chaz appeared as the love interest. Once Kristi accepted that Chaz—a modern day vampire and mobster from the 1920s—was in her story to stay, she realized she knew next to nothing about mobsters nor the era Chaz came from. And she got stuck.

To get unstuck, Kristi watched the movie *Mobsters* to get a fix on mobsters during the 1920s. After that she was able to expand to other mob movies from different eras, like *Casino* and *Goodfellas*, broadening her knowledge of what her mobster-vampire character might have experienced as he progressed through the decades to modern day.

Watching these movies worked so well to get her unstuck, Kristi now turns to film as a tool whenever she needs to learn new subject matter for her fiction, find inspiration, or stave off writer's block.

Fantasy author Todd Fahnestock was serenaded by writer's block over the entire course of writing his second published novel, *Mistress of Winter*. But he couldn't afford to get stuck—he was on a deadline. So he found a sure-fire way to re-inspire and re-invigorate himself whenever he heard the siren's song of writer's block: he watched recordings of the television series *Firefly* created by Joss Whedon. Todd has never met Mr. Whedon, yet Todd was so grateful for the inspiration that *Firefly* provided, he thanked him in the acknowledgements of *Mistress of Winter*.

Not that I can blame Todd—I can't help but be inspired by the genius of *Firefly* every time I watch an episode. However for me, *Firefly* is *too* good to work as a tool for getting unstuck. I get so lost in Whedon's story, I can never pull myself away to work on my own. Why is this bad? Remember what I told you: the minute you forget why you're doing this exercise is the minute it stops being an exercise.

As an aside I want to acknowledge that for some writers, watching a movie only serves to engage the inner critic, and thus this exercise is unlikely to work. For example, author and screenwriter Trai Cartwright says that watching movies "is just more work." When she gets jammed up on a story, instead of watching a movie she goes to a museum or art gallery.

> There's something about immersing myself in a different artistic process that loosens my brain up while feeding it at the same time.
> — Trai Cartwright, editor and screenwriting consultant

Similarly, newer writer John Pennington turns to other arts when he's stuck, but he takes a more hands-on approach: he paints. Dioramas, miniatures, landscapes—the "what" doesn't seem to matter. The act of painting helps free up his creativity and he's soon back to writing again.

47. HARMONIZE

Ask a writer about listening to music while writing and you're sure to get an opinion, usually a strong one.

"I must listen to music when I write."

"I can't listen to music when I write."

"I always listen to music, but only classical guitar."

"I never listen to music except when writing a fight scene, then heavy metal is a must."

What does music do for your writing? Does it bring harmony? Or discord?

Regardless of which camp you're in, what you *usually* do isn't the issue. If you're stuck, what you usually do isn't working. It's time for something different.

Try using music in a different way than you normally do. If you're a non-listener like me, try listening to music while you write to shake things up a bit. If you're still stuck, try a different song, a different type of music, or a different mode of employment (e.g. radio, CD, Web streaming). If you're a regular listener, try a different variety of music, or try silence (I can almost see you music-listening writers cringing at the thought!). The point is to change your musical writing routine.

Whether you typically write with music or without, any writer can benefit from the way music affects mood. Think about the scene you're stuck on. How is your point-of-view character feeling? What mood are you trying to evoke in the reader? Listening to music that evokes that feeling in you can often get you past the block.

> I love how music can instantly transport you and make you feel so many emotions. So when I'm stuck, I put on my playlist and remember what emotions I'm working to convey.
>
> – Cindi Madsen, *Resisting the Hero*

Jaxine Daniels uses this emotion-evoking technique in a very specific way: she selects a theme song for each book she writes. When she was writing her first novel, *Black Ice*, she played her theme song "Kokomo" by the Beach Boys whenever she got stuck. She'd close her eyes and sing along, allowing her sibling protagonists to come to life in her imagination. The song gave her a boost of emotion and placed her squarely in her characters' lives.

When Jaxine wrote the sequel, *Thin Ice*, the song "Kokomo" no longer worked. She discovered she needed a different song to reflect the new plot, theme, and emotions in the next book, and she found it in Matchbox Twenty's "If You're Gone."

Even years after writing that book, Jaxine says: "Just saying the song title makes my belly clench with the deep emotion that Grant feels in the black moments of that story."

For Jaxine, the theme song gives her a shove into the world of her characters. Once in that world, it's almost impossible for her to stay stuck. The theme song is her shortcut to the mental and emotional immersion in her story that she needs in order to keep cranking out words.

Sometimes, however, one song isn't enough. Authors Robin D. Owens and Cindi Madsen select multiple songs for one book.

> I try various things to become unstuck at various times. Currently I like the "making a soundtrack" approach. Sweeping themes that let me write, picking the right tune that reflects my hero and heroine: rock close to going over the top, but riding that sharp edge; cool, sophisticated jazz. Putting together the soundtrack helps me think of my characters, the beat of their lives, how they might handle the next crises. And can keep me writing to a beat, too.
>
> – Robin D. Owens, *Ghost Seer*

Cindi Madsen tailor-makes a playlist for each of her novels. Not only does she choose songs to fit the mood and theme of each story, she often selects individual songs to go with specific scenes. When the book is released, Cindi posts that book's playlist on her Website for readers who want to play the music that fits the story.

This is Cindi's playlist for *Falling for Her Fiancé,* a love story about two friends who fake their engagement:

"Ho Hey" – The Lumineers
"Blindsided" – Bon Iver
"My Life Would Suck Without You" – Kelly Clarkson
"My Body" – Young the Giant
"Stubborn Love" – The Lumineers
"Trojans" – Atlas Genius
"Afterlife" – Switchfoot
"It's Time" – Imagine Dragons
"Shattered" – O.A.R.
"Ready" – Kelly Clarkson
"Too Close" – Alex Clare
"She Is" – The Fray
"It Hurts" – Angels and Airwaves
"November Blue" – The Avett Brothers
"Long Shot" – Kelly Clarkson
"I'd Rather Be With You" – Joshua Radin
"Say When" – The Fray
"Sideways" – Citizen Cope
"I Want You" – Kelly Clarkson
"All I Need" – Mat Kearney
"Just You" – Amy Stroup
"All We Are" – Matt Nathanson
"Bloodstream" – Stateless
"Standing in Front of You" – Kelly Clarkson
"5:19" – Matt Wertz
"Running Back to You" – Matt Wertz

Cindi says that the last song, "Running Back to You," conveys the sentiment: *whatever happens, I am running back to you.* So when it came time to write and edit the big romantic gesture at the end of the book, she played that song and poured all the heightened emotion from the song into her writing.

Not only is listening to music a great way to slip into the writing zone and avoid getting stuck, it's also a formidable weapon for attacking writer's block when you find yourself stuck. Whatever music-listening camp you're in, give music a try.

48. STEP OUTSIDE

When you're stuck writing, one of the best things you can do is step outside.

When author Laura DiSilverio (aka Ella Barrick) gets stuck, her go-to solution is to head outside. Whatever the weather—wind, rain, sun or snow—she takes a long walk in the great outdoors. She says it never fails to blast the barriers away and get her writing.

So step outside. Take a deep, cleansing breath of outside air, go for a walk, do some gardening, or just sit. Whether you're in the big city or the suburbs, at the beach or in the woods, use all of your senses to take in the world around you.

It could be that all you needed was a little fresh air to feed the sputtering creative flame in your mind.

Are you refreshed and ready to go back to work now? Are you unstuck? If not, take this exercise a step further:

Look around you and imagine your character in that outdoor setting. What would she notice? What would she like and dislike about it? What would have prompted her to be there? What memories would it conjure? What regrets? What desires? What fears? Would she wish she were somewhere else?

Once you hit on a question that gets the gears turning in your head, roll with it. Don't stop to ask more questions. Let the thoughts, scenario, or dialogue play out in your imagination until you're so excited about an idea, you're dashing to write it.

For New York Times bestselling author Kevin J. Anderson, going outside to spend time with his characters is an important part of his process.

> I like to "get away" from real life and spend time in my fictional universes with my imaginary friends. Too many distractions at home, and I love to go out to walk, to move, to receive input in all five senses as I walk on trails, even on tame bike paths. It allows me to THINK, to have quiet time with my characters, to save the world (or, in certain circumstances, destroy it). Walking on a trail is like pacing around a room—a time-proven method for pondering—but a thousand times better. Especially if you live in beautiful Colorado.
>
> – Kevin J. Anderson, author of
> more than 120 published books

Whether you step outside to visit with your imaginary friends or just to get a little fresh air, abandoning your desk for the great outdoors can clear away the cobwebs and get you writing again.

49. DUMP YOUR JUNK

This exercise asks you to dump a "junk drawer," but the point of this exercise is not to get the drawer clean. The point is to approach it from the perspective of your story, of your characters. What would the drawer contents tell you about your protagonist (or antagonist) if it was his/her junk? What would it tell you about your story world? How does it fit into your genre? Is your story futuristic—does your character see the junk as artifacts? Is it a mystery—is your character looking for a clue to a disappearance? Is it young adult—is your teen character looking for money in his big sister's drawer?

Try not to think about sorting the junk to put away. Try not to think of it as *your* junk. Try not to look at it *as yourself* at all. Instead, let your mind wander where it will, while holding the intent of the exercise loosely in your mind and staying within the parameters of your story.

THINK: Why would my character have a golf ball in her junk drawer? Who golfs? If she's the golfer, is she any good? Where does she golf and how often? How long has she been playing? Did she have lessons? Who does she golf with? Is it difficult for her to afford? Has she ever had aspirations of making it more than a hobby (instructor, professional, competitive team)? Why does she golf? Is her reason for golfing now different from the reason she took up golfing to begin with? Does it relax her or is she really intense about it? Is it a recreation she looks forward to? Does she use it to escape her problems? Does she yearn for it when she can't go? Does she feel guilty about not golfing more often because of the financial investment she's made in it? Why is the ball in this drawer rather than in her golf bag? Is she normally lazy or disorganized, or did an event cause her to toss the ball there rather than put it away? Or, if it's not her ball, whose is it? Did it belong to her dad who died last year? An ex-boyfriend or girlfriend? Is it evidence her estranged teenaged son has been back uninvited when she's not home? What emotions/memories/thoughts does it bring up about the owner of the ball?

DO NOT THINK: Why didn't this ball get put where it belongs? I really must be better about that (or get on my roommate's/spouse's/kid's case about that); I'll take it to the garage now and put it where it belongs; oh gee, the garage/golf bag/gardening/laundry/dog needs to be attended to...

When Jennifer Lovett Herbranson was drafting *Redemption*, she began her story with the protagonist, Lane, leaving her abusive husband and embarking on a new life. But she got stuck on what to show next—Lane arriving at her new home so depressed she can't do anything, or six months later after Lane's had time to collect herself.

In the hope of gaining some clarity on this dilemma, Jennifer dumped a junk drawer, pretending the contents were from Lane's new life. She found several items that showed the relationships and activities important to Lane after six months in her new home:

- supplies for building mini-greenhouses—a project she does with her daughter;
- a mortar and pestle her grandmother gave her for grinding herbs grown in the greenhouses;
- string her new boyfriend uses when building forts with her daughter.

Since Lane left her husband abruptly with no more than a suitcase, Jennifer decided there would be nothing in the drawer that the character had brought from her previous life. So Jennifer was surprised to discover "evidence" of the character's backstory:

- scissors left in the drawer as a quick-access weapon to protect herself;
- candy—a deliberate way to spite her ex-husband who never let her have anything "unhealthy;"
- the cake knife from her wedding buried under the rest of the junk; her mother brought it over trying to be kind, but Lane hid it because any reminder of   her previous marriage sends her into a panic attack.

Jennifer says this exercise was great for exploring a character's relationships with the people and things around him/her. It helped her see that her character would still carry scars from her old life—internal wounds that would be evident in the items around her—even six months after leaving her husband.

But more than that, it helped Jennifer discover ways to show her character's past within the context of the present. It got her unstuck because she realized that she could "skip to the part of the story where readers can really root for Lane" without having to show the drudgery and depression of the six months leading up to that point.

50. FIND YOUR ZEN

There are many methods for centering oneself and clearing the mind, from the new age to the time-honored and ancient. For writers, seeking clarity of mind through a meditative state is not only a great way to get unstuck, it's a great way to prevent getting stuck in the first place. From praying to yoga to howling at the moon, there's something to help everyone get in The Zone.

I wasn't kidding about the "howling." Julia S. Pierce gets ready to write each day with fifteen minutes of meditation, followed by a quick session of howling with her dog, P.J. For Julia this not only clears her mind and gets her blood flowing, it invariably makes her laugh, which puts her in the right mindset for her playful, puppy-filled story, *The Land of Yay.*

Meditation (typically without the howling) is a common way for writers, as well as all sorts of artists and creative types, to achieve clarity and induce a state of mind where creativity flows. Prolific writer Barbara Samuel (who is also published under Barbara O'Neal and Ruth Wind) employs a specific type—guided meditation:

The ways I use guided meditation for writing are numerous. There is a particular one I like to use when I'm feeling depleted, imagining myself going to the meadow where there is a cottage where I can find rest and inspiration, whatever I need. (Just writing that makes me take a deep, calming breath.) It's a magical place, this mental cottage, surrounded by quiet and safety and a thick, nourishing forest. Inside is a big room with a kitchen and bookshelves and a bed for sleeping and a comfortable desk and chair by the fire, looking out to a window that seems to look out to whatever I need on a given day. I only need to spend ten minutes there to feel refreshed.

– Barbara O'Neal,
The All You Can Dream Buffet

For journalist and memoir writer Charise Simpson, yoga is her mind-clearing method of choice. She finds that when she's stuck it's almost always because she's distracted, so when she feels herself struggling to write she knows it's time to do some yoga and regain her focus.

Twenty minutes of Sun Salutations will usually do the trick. It's important to set your intention before you start, however. I usually "intend" to clear my mind and open my creative channels. It may be a bit woo-woo for some people, but I love it and it works.

I start slowly, working through the first few poses, then move on to a full salutation cycle. Finally I add in Warrior Poses 1-3, making them increasingly harder each time. Balancing poses like "tree" and "crow" are really good for me because they require focus to do them successfully.

Also, it's very important to breathe correctly during the Sun Salutations, and to do 3-5 minutes of Ujjayi breathing, or "ocean breathing" in addition to that. Ujjayi breathing actually changes the chemistry of your brain, taking the energy away from the anxiety focused amygdala, and moving it toward more creative/productive areas. A psychologist actually proved this to me with her fancy-schmancy biofeedback machine.

Yoga gets the blood flowing, changes the brain chemistry, and balances you overall. For me, it makes me feel good and it restores my focus so I can write again.

–Charise Simpson,
Riding the Chicken Train

You can take advantage of any type of meditative practice to achieve a clear head and ready yourself for writing. But you don't have to stop there. You can also use these methods to open your mind to gifts and messages from your spiritual guides, explore story and character options, or use the opportunity to directly address an area where you're stuck.

Visualization can be a great tool for facing head-on "what should happen next" in your story. For writer Matt Bille, when he's blocked as to the next plot twist, he reads his last chapter while visualizing himself in a movie theater watching the story unfold on the screen. When he gets to the part of the story where he stopped writing, he imagines what he'd see happening next in the movie. For Lynda Hilburn, she visualizes holding her finished book in her hand, and looking through it to see what she decided to do at the stuck place.

Similarly, when you're meditating, doing yoga, howling, or visiting your "cottage in a meadow," you can think about the point in your story where you are stuck. Ask yourself questions about your story, explore possible solutions, even ask your characters to help you get unstuck. The clarity of mind, the positive attitude, and the openness to creativity brought about by a meditative state can help you get unstuck and stay that way.

51. Zzzzzz

It may sound crazy, but sleeping can help you get unstuck. No, really.

When you are in a state somewhere between fully awake and fully asleep, your brain can do amazing things.

> The twilight between wakefulness and sleep is a wonderful time to ponder every aspect of the story, to try to get at the "truth" of my story. What would the characters really do in this situation?
>
> – Barbara Nickless,
> "Suffer the Children," *Future Americas*

So when you're drifting off to sleep or just waking, ask yourself about your story, like "what should happen next? " You can even ask "why am I stuck at such-and-such place?" You can also ask your characters things like "what do you most want?" or "why do you refuse to do X when I really need you to do X" and "what would you rather do?"

It's not only that "twilight" phase that can help you get unstuck. Sleep itself can lead to a breakthrough.

For example, the original idea for Kristi Helvig's novel *Burn Out* first came to her in a dream. So when she got stuck at a critical plot point at the climax of the story, she decided to take a nap and see if her subconscious could figure out what should happen next. Sure enough, she dreamt the solution, then jumped out of bed and wrote the scene.

So when you're stumped as to what should happen next in your story, try taking a nap. If you're not a good napper, like me, use your regular sleep time to put your half-conscious and/or subconscious mind to work on your story.

52. RETREAT! RETREAT!

We've all heard about fabulous writing retreats where every need is provided for, and all that's required of you is to write. It's a fabulous way to get down to business and concentrate one hundred percent on your story. Giving your work this undivided focus is an excellent way to get unstuck.

There are lots of retreat opportunities available to writers, so if you find one you can afford, go for it! But what if you can't afford one? Believe it or not, a retreat doesn't have to be expensive. If you create your own retreat, you can spend as much or as little money as you want. It doesn't have to be fancy. You don't even necessarily have to *go* anywhere. As multi-published author Jennie Marts has found, a retreat can be as simple as changing your frame of mind:

> Having a writer's retreat is simply taking a mental and sometimes physical break from the ordinary way that you write. It's putting yourself in a different frame of mind, and often a different locale.
>
> – Jennie Marts,
> *Easy Like Sunday Mourning*

The basis of "retreating" is to immerse yourself in an environment where you don't have to think about anything or do anything other than write. The trick to creating your own retreat is carving out a place and time you can dedicate to writing, and then planning and preparing in advance so you have the fewest possible distractions and interruptions.

One of the best things I ever did for my writing was to stage my own retreat. When I was mired in revisions on my first novel, I felt so hopelessly stuck I considered throwing in the towel. Instead I decided the story was worth one last valiant attempt at redemption. But *what*?

I knew that if I was to have any hope of finding the true core of the story and stripping away all the chaff, I needed to focus on my writing in a way that seemed impossible in my busy day-to-day life. Something drastic was called for. So I did something drastic. I got rid of my family.

In actuality what happened was I asked my husband (okay, begged and bribed) to take our small children to see his parents for Spring Break, which would give me a full ten days alone to focus on my revisions. He agreed on one condition: I had to "finish the damn book."

Talk about pressure! But pressure—and pure focus—turned out to be exactly what I needed.

The pressure began the week before my retreat. I worked like a dog to prep my life for ten days of pure, uninterrupted writing. I stocked up on frozen dinners, snacks, disposable plates and cups, and every other provision I thought necessary, including plenty of coffee. I washed all my favorite comfy clothes. I returned emails I knew wouldn't wait, cancelled all appointments for Spring Break week, and took care of every regular chore that could be done in advance. (Who cares if the trash can sits at the curb for ten days? Not me!)

Next I contacted my supervisor and coworkers at my job (which at the time was a nearly full-time volunteer gig for a nonprofit) and told them that I needed ten days of "no contact." We identified the tasks I had to complete prior to the retreat, postponed the rest, and designated a pinch-hitter to cover any emergencies in my department that came up while I was away. I realize that this sort of clean break from a job (paid or otherwise) isn't easy, but if you really want a retreat, find a way to use comp time or vacation days to gain a period of "no contact." Certainly you could swing a three-day weekend if you put your mind to it.

Finally I had "the talk" with my friends, neighbors, and extended family. I told them my plan for the retreat and made them promise not to call me, stop by, or expect email replies during that time period. Everyone was on board, but my mother needed some convincing. Her fear was that I'd fall down the stairs, break a leg, and lie there suffering for a week before someone found me. So I agreed to a very brief "daily check in" with her so she knew I was okay. That, along with a promise that my neighbors would watch my house for fire, did the trick.

When I first sent my kids out the door to their grandparents' house, I didn't know what to do with myself. The quiet was astounding. I was paralyzed. For about three seconds. Then I took a giant mug of steaming java to my office and got to work. By the time my husband's car left our cul-de-sac, I was already deep in my fictional world playing with my imaginary friends.

I lived an entire lifetime in those ten days. I found the core of my story. I found the deep hidden truth of my protagonist. I found the soft, gooey inside of my antagonist. I discovered plot twists and turns that I didn't realize my subconscious had planted. I experienced more "aha" moments than I'd had during the *years* I'd spent on that story up to that point. And I finished the revisions a few minutes before my family walked back in the door. It was the best thing I'd ever written, and I felt proud and accomplished and smart. Even though that novel ended up tucked away unseen by the free world, that doesn't take away from the glory and satisfaction and benefit of the experience.

I wish there were some way for me to convey to you the degree to which that retreat changed me as a writer. But I don't think any words I put on the page will do the experience justice. Alas, you will just have to try it for yourself.

Here are some options for a do-it-yourself retreat. You'll be surprised how little they can cost and how much you have to gain.

- If you have a job outside the home, consider writing at work after-hours, especially if that job is in an office, or the jobsite has an office space or conference room. Many workplaces have all the necessities if not the comforts of home. If the jobsite is closed all weekend or over a holiday break, even better.

- Go camping or get a motel or hotel room. A Bed & Breakfast can be a lovely option.

- Send your family on a trip without you (but if you choose to stay at home, you must be disciplined about not doing housework or succumbing to other distractions).

- House-sit for a friend or for hire. You'll have all the comforts of home, but none of your own "shoulds." You may have to do a few chores for your out-of-town host, like watering the plants or feeding the fish, but the laundry isn't yours, you don't need to scrub the tub, you've come armed with your own food so you don't need to shop, the filing's not yours, the bills aren't yours—the only thing you *should* be doing is writing.

Since my original Spring Break retreat, I've sent my family away several more times with the same rewarding results. I've learned that this kind of focused, extended binge-writing works so well for me, I try to do it at least once a year.

While I'll always enjoy retreating at home, I've also found I like to tag along with my husband when he goes on a business trip. I get tons of writing done in a beautiful hotel all day, with evening breaks for dinner with my husband. When I truly need 24/7 focus and I can't arrange to stay home alone, house-sitting for a friend is the next best thing. I've also tried a variety of "official" writing retreats, and there are definitely times when surrounding myself with other working writers— and being able to brainstorm and share—is the best way for me to get unstuck.

A week-long retreat can be a marvelous way to get through a big block, but don't feel you need a long period of time in order for this retreat exercise to work. Even a few well-orchestrated hours with the right mindset can provide the uninterrupted focus you need to get unstuck.

CONCLUSION

The Bottom Line

You don't have to be stuck.

No writer has to be at the mercy of writer's block. In many cases it's possible to *prevent* writer's block from rearing its ugly head by prepping your life for writing—treating writing with the consideration you would any other job, organizing your life to accommodate, setting clear expectations for yourself and your loved ones, and then showing up for work.

If despite these faithful efforts you do find yourself stuck, you don't have to stay that way. Don't believe anyone who tells you otherwise. Writer's block can be formidable, but you're not powerless against it. There's no reason to sit back and take it—take charge and do something about it.

With this book you have 52 weapons at your disposal, so when writer's block does rear its ugly head, go on the offensive. Attack. Beat it back, then keep it at bay. Because you're a writer. You need to write. Readers need to see your words. Let's not keep them waiting.

The Moral of This Story

I bet you thought the moral of the story was "you don't have to be stuck." No, silly, that's the bottom line. The moral of the story is *you don't have to go it alone.*

Writing is heralded as a solitary endeavor as often as writer's block is painted as an omnipotent and inevitable woe. But the writing life doesn't have to be solitary any more than writer's block has to be debilitating.

Did you notice how many of the exercises in this book involve reaching out to others for support, advice, expertise, inspiration, or help? Four of the five "life prep" activities in Part One and nearly half of the 52 exercises suggest working with others or have an example of someone who did.

This book itself is a great example of not going it alone. I connected with other writers for every single portion of this book. I built the foundation by learning from other writers—reading their words, taking classes and workshops, attending conferences and retreats, and participating in critique groups, goals groups, and improv writing groups. For the information contained in these pages, writers provided ideas, resources, examples, and anecdotes, not to mention testing the exercises. That doesn't even begin to cover mentoring, inspiration, brainstorming, proofreading—the list goes on. And we're not just talking about my writer-friends, critique partners, and publishing team. My family and non-writing friends were a big part of this endeavor, too, and I could not have done it without their encouragement and support.

Even though I do sit at my computer and write all by myself, I never feel like I'm in this writing life alone. You're not alone either. You now have this book full of advice and exercises—complete with the wisdom and anecdotes of dozens of other working writers—that you can turn to any time you need.

But don't stop there. Reach out to others, make connections, build a base of support. You and your writing will benefit, this I can promise.

Next Steps
Now that you've conquered writer's block, there's nothing in the way of you completing the next great novel or work of nonfiction, right? Perhaps. Perhaps not.

See, writer's block is not the only demon we writers face. We also have to do battle with procrastination, perfectionism, fear, and fatalism, not to mention tackling beasts like editing and marketing.

Right now I'm busy marshaling anecdotes and exercises for more books in the "52 Ways" series to help you slay your writing demons, build worlds and characters, edit your books to a professional polish, and market the heck out of them, too.

If you'd like to join forces in this battle against writing challenges of all kinds, visit **www.ChrisMandeville.com** to learn new tips and anecdotes, and perhaps share some of your own.

Why join forces? Because—say it with me now—we don't have to go it alone.

APPENDIX A: USING A DECK OF CARDS

Get a deck of playing cards. Any standard deck of cards will work. Remove all the "extra" cards, like the Jokers.

To select an exercise at random, pull a card from the deck and match the card to the exercise on the following list.

If you'd like to target a category or categories to draw from, separate the corresponding suit or suits from your deck of cards, then draw randomly from this subset.

Note: if you discover or create exercises not covered in this book that you want to include in your "deck," you can assign them to the Joker and other extra cards that typically accompany a new pack of cards.

SPADES - The Right Place at the Write Time
HEARTS - Character Juice
DIAMONDS - Story Mechanics
CLUBS - Mind Openers—Getting in The Zone

CARD   EXERCISE

♠ SPADES ♠

ACE 1
2 2
3 3
4 4
5 5
6 6
7 7
8 8
9 9
10 10
JACK 11
QUEEN 12
KING 13

♥ HEARTS ♥

ACE 14
2 15
3 16
4 17
5 18
6 19
7 20
8 21
9 22
10 23
JACK 24
QUEEN 25
KING 26

CARD   EXERCISE

♦ DIAMONDS ♦

♣ CLUBS ♣

APPENDIX B: CHARACTER PROFILE

CHARACTER PROFILE
from Laura Hayden's
"Left-Brain–Right Brain/Creativity Program"
suspense@suspense.net
http:suspense.net

You may distribute this profile, but please give Laura Hayden credit as the source and include the above e-mail and web address on ALL copies.

Part One: Personal Profile

Name:

Age:

Birth Date:

Birthplace:

Hair:

Eyes:

Height:

Weight:

Other Facial Features/Appearance Details:

Dress (style, colors):

Description Of Home:

Dominant Character Trait:

Secondary Character Trait:
(contrast with dominant)

Best Friend:

Other Friends:

Enemies and Why:

Family:

What kind of person is character with others: (name persons and describe interaction)

Sees self as:

Is seen by others as:

Sense of humor:

Temper:

Basic nature:

Ambitions:

Educational background:

Work experience:

Philosophy of life:

Habits:

Talents (when character looks good):

Hobbies/pastimes:

Choice of entertainments:

What trait will make character come alive?

Why is character likeable?

Why is character loveable?

Part Two: Personal Interview– Answer in Character's Voice

Occupation:

Current Home:

Marital Status:

Children:

Favorite Pig Out Food:

Favorite Performer/Author/Sportsman, Etc:

Every New Year's Eve I Resolve To:

Nobody Knows I Am:

I Wish I Could Stop:

I'm A Sucker For:

The Worst Part Of My Life Is:

I Want To Teach My Children That:

A Good Time For Me Is:

The Worst Advice That My Father Gave Me Was:

I Thought I Was Grown Up When:

When I Feel Sorry For Myself I:

Nobody Would Believe Me If They Saw Me:

My Friends Like Me Because:

My Pet Peeve Is:

My Major Accomplishment:

I Can Die Happy When:

I'd Really Rather:

My Most Humbling Experience Was:

REFERENCES

Baty, Chris, *No Plot? No Problem!: A Low-Stress, High-Velocity Guide to Writing a Novel in 30 Days*, Chronicle Books 2004

Campbell, Joseph, *The Hero with a Thousand Faces*, Bollingen Series/Princeton University Press 1973

Dixon, Debra, *GMC: Goal, Motivation, and Conflict*, Gryphon Books For Writers 1996

Sams, Jamie and Carson, David, *Medicine Cards: the Discovery of Power Through the Ways of Animals*, Bear & Company 1988

Staw, Jane Anne, Ph.D., *Unstuck: A Supportive and Practical Guide to Working Through Writer's Block*, St. Martin's Griffin 2005

Swain, Dwight V., *Techniques of the Selling Writer*, University of Oklahoma Press 1981

Vogler, Christopher, *The Writer's Journey Mythic Structure for Writers, Second Edition*, Michael Wiese Productions 1998

INDEX

F

G

H

I

Made in the USA
Lexington, KY
22 June 2016